10

SOCIAL MOVEMENTS
IN THE UNITED STATES

Studies
in Sociology

Social Movements in the United States

C. WENDELL KING
University of Massachusetts

Random House

NEW YORK

PREFACE

Social movements constitute a significant subject for sociology. Their sociological legitimacy is evident enough in that movements involve group-shared behavior and thought as well as regularly defined social relationships. The significance of social movements lies partly in the fact that they have become a prominent characteristic of modern mass societies; they contribute to the structural complexity of these societies while being, at the same time, a product of that complexity. But their significance does not depend solely on their prominence or prevalence, for they have a very definite relevance for two other areas of sociological study: one, largely theoretical, is the field of social change and the other, largely practical in its implications, is social planning. Whatever light the present work may throw on social movements should also help illuminate a little these other, broader areas.

This dual relevance of the study of movements becomes apparent in several ways. In the first place, social movements themselves involve one type of social planning, and movements are one kind of agency for deliberately altering the social order and for attempting to predetermine events and situations of the future. To the extent that social planning operates on the basis of principles more efficient than trial-and-error, to the degree that it is guided by something more effective than sheer idealism—to that extent it must draw upon scientifically established findings, some of which can be derived from the study of social movements.

In the second place, the study of movements has a

v

relevance for the field of social change because movements
are both a manifestation and an agency of change. The objectives which they seek to realize involve modifying existing social arrangements in one way or another, and therefore observing their activities can be instructive for the
theoretical problem of how effectively the course of social
change can be deliberately guided and by what techniques
and mechanisms. Furthermore, movements themselves
constitute new social items whose careers are presumably
subject to the same processes and influences as other social
innovations. Because of these relationships between social
movements and social change, several concepts and principles already developed in the area of change have been
used in this study to highlight certain phases of the subject
at hand.

As a matter of fact, movements are treated in the present
study almost entirely in the broad context of social change,
either explicitly or implicitly, although an understanding
of movements and an appreciation of their significance may
be quite possible in some other context. My point of view
in this matter accounts for the organization revealed by the
table of contents. Following the first two chapters, which
suggest something of the nature of movements and the
societies in which they occur, the problem dominating the
remaining chapters is: what happens to a movement once
it is initiated? From this general question, more specific
ones such as these follow: As an evolving social novelty,
to what processes is the movement subjected because of its
inherent nature and because of reactions invariably evoked
in groups and individuals by innovations? How do its own
component elements influence its growth or decline as a
social system? What aspects of the external social setting
are especially influential in this respect? The last chapter,
however, is a kind of epilogue, a dash of cold water on

reader optimism and on any unguarded tendencies by the author to make things seem too pat.

In a brief study of a broad subject, extensive documentation is impossible. But three American movements in particular have been introduced to illustrate various concepts and generalizations: the Grange, Christian Science, and the Ku Klux Klan. Other movements would have served as well; these were chosen somewhat arbitrarily except for the deliberate effort to secure three movements very unlike each other. Moral Rearmament, Father Divine's Peace Mission, and the Birth Control Movement have also been drawn upon for occasional illustration.

Though help and influence have come from many sources, I wish to express my special indebtedness to three colleagues: to A. G. Keller of Yale University for his exposition as teacher and writer of the dynamic attributes of society, to Edmund Volkart of Stanford University and to J. Henry Korson and Mary Goss of the University of Massachusetts for reading the manuscript and for their discerning comments, and to Charles H. Page of Smith College for his friendly but firm guidance and criticism. And I am particularly grateful to my wife, Marjorie, for her help in preparing the manuscript and for her forbearance during the entire period of incubation.

C. WENDELL KING

CONTENTS

1 Mass Society and Social Movements

Although the accounts of specific social movements usually center around their leaders and founders, the sociologist's concern is chiefly with movements as a whole and the social settings in which they occur. Accordingly, the general emphasis of the present study is on groups rather than individuals. Nevertheless the significance of the modern individual's needs and dissatisfactions must be recognized from the beginning. These psychological elements are admittedly elusive—as is the whole problem of human personality—and the conditions which induce people to join a wide variety of movements are often obscure. Yet any attempt to account for the startling multiplicity of movements in contemporary society without reference to motives, satisfactions, and frustrations can only result in a description which is incomplete and unrealistic. Of the characteristically human requirements or needs, a few can be tentatively related to movement participation. Furthermore, there are conditions of life in modern mass society which no doubt accentuate these requirements and complicate the individual's struggle for satisfactions. To identify some of the important connections between such conditions and the proliferation of social movements is an important sociological task.

The Mass Society

The *mass society* is easier to illustrate than to define. A good example is the American society as contained in the United States. On a more limited scale, any large American city bears the characteristics associated with this concept. People are differentiated on the bases of age, sex, marital status, and kinship in all societies, but in a mass society additional social distinctions are found. It contains subgroups based on occupation, wealth, locality, social class, political affiliation, and perhaps race, religion and nationality. A mass society is, above all, heterogeneous and not merely big. Along with this heterogeneity there is an emphasis on organization and a large variety of formal associations. Although personal relationships persist, especially in the family and the clique, they tend to be replaced by some that are formalized and impersonal. Human contacts are likely to be casual and transitory rather than intimate and enduring.

With the diversity of subgroups there is a diversity of codes of behavior and systems of belief. This is not to say that members of a mass society have no values or mores in common, but there are fewer common denominators than in the folk society. In short, the number of cultural traits shared by the members of a society tends to vary inversely with the number of subgroups in that society.

Social movements, of course, are not confined to the mass society. Religious movements with messianic overtures, for example, have frequently appeared in American Indian tribes since their contact with the white man.[1] The existence of Buddhism, Islam, and Christianity is sufficient evidence that social movements antedate mass societies; other less ancient examples can be drawn from pre-industrial Europe and America.

But a spectacular abundance of social movements marks the society whose traditions have been shaken by industrial urbanism and whose structure is scarred by cleavages between diverse groups. Except for the modern nations where authoritarian governments exercise maximum supervision and suppression, a correlation exists between mass societies and social movements. Thus in the United States, the post-Civil War period provides an almost endless catalog of movements which reached various stages of growth and professed a wide variety of goals: for example, the Knights of Labor, the Know Nothings, Populism, the Grangers, Feminism, Moral Rearmament, the Ku Klux Klan, Technocracy, Prohibitionism, Christian Science, and the Townsend Plan.

Circumstances Conducive to Movements

Since social movements are phenomena of the past as well as of the present, some circumstances conducive to movements have existed rather continuously. Our concern here, however, is with certain conditions which appear to be particularly associated with the recent proliferation of movements: cultural confusion, social heterogeneity, individual discontent, and mass communication.

Cultural Confusion When a person is implored by one agency to save his money through investment in government bonds, by another to set it aside in insurance policies, and by still another to spend it on the latest model of refrigerator or washing machine, his situation contains a measure of inconsistency. Confusions in a modern-day culture, however, involve more than a clash of slogans, more than a blatant competition for the consumer's attention.

Urban government operates by the machine method with modest to exorbitant indulgence in graft while the family solemnly tries to inculcate in the young the value of honesty, which in turn is often rather loosely defined in the arena of industrial competition. Business interests insist on the protection of their private property, but at the same time neighborhood play groups may be equally insistent on stealing as a test for membership eligibility. The teacher may espouse some postulate of science branded as atheistic by a religious order, which is simultaneously finding its opposition to divorce undercut by state legislation and the courts. Such disparity of norms can be illustrated at length.

The cultural elements and sanctioning agencies that fail to contribute toward the cohesion of the society have been appropriately labeled dysfunctional.[2] Admittedly, dysfunctional traits may be found in primitive and folk cultures. But from the viewpoint of most individuals in these less complex communities, there is a consistency and wholeness in the way of life of their group that gives an impression of regularity and pattern. For most questions there are unequivocal answers, and the cultural universals, the norms and values to which most adults in the society subscribe, are many and powerful.

The mass society presents a dramatic contrast. Here are relatively few universals on which all the society's members agree. Answers to socially relevant questions may conflict, depending on who does the answering, or they may be hedged with qualifications. In many problem situations the individual is offered alternative solutions with undefined or ill-defined consequences; in other situations there may be weak norms for guidance or none at all. This lack of agreement on standards, and on the interpretation of standards, is revealed not only by the findings of public opinion polls but by the very existence of such polls. If the members of a mass society were largely in agreement, the polls could not survive since their results would be known by everyone in advance.[3]

To norms loaded with equivocation, to agencies often working at cross-purposes, to cultural vagaries and contradictions—to these must be added rapid change as one more complication for the dweller in modern society. Even elements of the culture which are not clearly dysfunctional may drop by the way or have their place in the culture changed, their meaning altered. Although the most rapid and frequent changes seem to occur in the area of fads, more fundamental beliefs such as those pertaining to chaperonage, educational aims and methods, and even definitions of national loyalty can also undergo modification in a startlingly short time.

Inconsistency and instability, then, are primary marks of a mass society. They are cross-currents which engulf its members. Numerous public and private counseling services, the themes of dramas and soap operas and novels, the popularity of self-help books— these are both evidence and by-products of "the rootlessness of the lives of many of us, the feeling of unconnectedness and unworthiness. . . ."[4] The proliferation of social movements is no less a consequence. Cultural confusions and vacuums create an atmosphere conducive to even the most bizarre proposals, many of which thrive and grow. Providing answers and offering durable ideals are part of "the promise" of many movements. However illusive that promise may ultimately be, the impression it gives of consistency and stability often has great appeal.

Social Heterogeneity and Organization Many, though not all, of the cultural ambiguities and contradictions of a mass society stem from its heterogeneity. American society, for example, is made up of various religious and ethnic groups, of wage earners and employers, of several social classes, of farmers and factory workers. This multiplicity of groups means that some areas of American life are characterized not by a single code of behavior but by a diversity of codes. Within the broad framework of such American universals as beliefs in democracy, monotheism, monogamy, and personal freedom and opportunity, there is room for much backing and filling, for sharp contrasts in values and norms, and, significantly, for variety in the interpretation of the universals themselves. No individual can or does subscribe to all these codes of behavior; he will even be completely unaware of some. His reactions will range from enthusiastic support through indifference to violent opposition.

With clashes of opinion come conflicts of power in the effort to put opinion into action. In a mass society, even to bring one's beliefs and proposals into that vague arena called public opinion, simply to get a hearing, calls for elaborate activities. Rousing the apathetic and counteracting the antagonistic are even more difficult matters for the subgroups in such a society.

Organization is an essential instrument for such subgroups. It is a means for overcoming the paucity of personal contacts. It facilitates the search for supporters and the identification of opponents whose activities may be obscure or elusive. It is useful in reaching legislators and other influential persons, who frequently seem able to hear only the loudest—or best organized—chorus of voices. Whether as political parties, labor unions, secular appendages of churches, farm blocs, or in a hundred other forms, the organized association is chiefly an offspring of the mass society.

Since modern social movements appear, in some stage of their development, as formal associations, the multiplicity of such movements is not surprising. Not only are there many subgroups and hence many special interests and a variety of values around which growth can occur. There are also numerous obstacles to realizing these interests and values, and these are virtually insuperable without the use of techniques possible only through organization.

Individual Discontent The general term "discontent" is used deliberately here since any of its specific aspects may be in part a consequence of living in a mass society: anxiety about the future, frustration in the present, continuing tensions from unsatisfied desires, or bewilderment arising from inexplicable situations. Social movements—along with other manifestations of change—are commonly ascribed to "social unrest." [5] This unrest is the product of discontent in a great many individual human beings. It becomes discernible when enough individuals give overt expression to their dissatisfaction. To say that social unrest is conducive to the appearance of social movements is to say, in a sense, that large numbers of people are seeking answers they do not have, reassurance that the answers they do have are right, or ways of implementing the answers of whose rightness they are convinced.

It has been suggested that social heterogeneity and cultural confusion contribute to individual discontent.

Margaret Mead, the anthropologist, illustrates the point in describing the dilemmas of the twentieth-century American woman:

> So a girl's father may be a Presbyterian, an imperialist, a vegetarian, a teetotaler, with a strong literary preference for Edmund Burke, a believer in the open shop and a high tariff, who believes that a woman's place is in the home, that young girls should wear corsets, not roll their stockings, nor go riding with young men in the evening. But her mother's father may be a Low Episcopalian, a believer in high living, a strong advocate of States' Rights and the Monroe Doctrine, who reads Rabelais, likes to go to musical shows and horse races. . . . Her mother is of a quietistic frame of mind, very much interested in Indian philosophy, a pacifist, a strict non-participator in life, who in spite of her daughter's devotion to her will not make any move to enlist her enthusiasms. And this may be within the girl's own household. Add to it the groups represented, advocated, defended by her friends, her teachers, and the books which she reads by accident, and the list of possible enthusiasm, of suggested allegiances incompatible with one another, becomes appalling.[6]

Weak cultural integration can impinge on the individual in a number of ways. Only a few of the more apparent consequences have been selected for discussion here. Some involve a generalized "desire for meaning"; others result in relatively specific dilemmas concerning the individual's conception of himself and his status, the values he cherishes, and the achievements to which he aspires.

In the first place, the values and ideals derived by the individual in a mass society from one or more of his subgroups are sometimes disparaged or opposed by other subgroups. This consequence of diverse codes has already been illustrated in the discussion of social heterogeneity, but the additional case of "native Americanism" may be cited. Many people of Old American (Scotch-Irish and English) stock in the United States feel that aliens and citizens of recent foreign ancestry are interlopers, indifferent to the national welfare at best and untrustworthy or traitorous at worst. That this idealization of long, native genealogy is hardly shared by the "newcomers" merely heightens anxieties and animosities in the Old Americans. Sporadic intensification of this uneasiness is revealed in the popularity of such movements as the Ku Klux Klan, Know Nothings, and other organizations which exploit "nativism."

A second circumstance which can generate personal discontent is one in which the individual's status (or his feelings about it) is recognized but nominally or not at all by other groups.[7] This is essentially a special case of the situation noted above since some of a person's values will inevitably pertain to his place in the society—and if an individual's own conception of his status is not shared by others, the result can be psychological torture. The connection between the tendency to cherish nativism and the feeling that Old Americans should be granted deference by other ethnic groups is apparent. Another example is the farmer's self-evaluation as "the backbone of the nation," a claim which elicits less than hearty agreement from the miner or the factory worker. The growth of the Grange and other rural organizations was encouraged partly by the farmer's earlier failures in securing recognition.

Third, an individual's goals may be opposed by members of other groups, especially when his goals violate the values of such groups or of the society in general. The nativist finds that his objective, say, of deporting "foreigners" or keeping them politically and economically impotent runs headlong into American ideals of personal freedom and achievement. Too, an individual's aims may conflict not only with the general attitudes but also with the specific goals of other groups. The super-patriot's aims to suppress or repatriate others are clearly at odds with the aims of minorities to remain here and to attain economic success, political participation, and social acceptance.

Finally, there are situations in which the individual's goals, seemingly unopposed, still elude realization for one or both of two reasons. On the one hand, failure may stem from personal inadequacy or fortuitous circumstances. The plight of an economically insecure farmer may be due to his own lack of skill; it may also be due, however, to a nationwide depression or a decline in the price of his products. A second—and more provocative—reason for the inability of the individual to attain his ends is the absence or inadequacy of socially defined means to those ends. This problematical relationship between means and ends is called *anomie*.[8] The ultimate goal of economic success—as an example —was dangled before the American farmer in the nineteenth century, but the prerequisite to achieving prosperity—reasonable costs of farm machinery, credit, and especially transportation—were often beyond his grasp. Eventually, of course, many farmers were able through organized action to pave legislative avenues that led more closely to their objectives.

The individual does not always understand or recognize the "real" reasons why his aims are unfulfilled. He is often bewildered, confused, knowing something is wrong but not knowing why. Caught in such situations many individuals experience a strong "desire for meaning." [9] While this desire involves to some extent an individual's conception of himself and the enhancement of that conception, it is not so much a matter of specific

frustrations as of a vague feeling of uneasiness and ap-
prehension. This feeling stems from an absence of
ready-made interpretations of problems and situations.
Some people can ignore such problems and retreat
mentally from the situation; for others, however, the
consequence is tension and dissatisfaction until interpretations (and they need not be scientifically valid)
are somehow found.

The desire for meaning would seem indeed to be virtually inevitable for many individuals in the mass society with its cultural inconsistencies and confusions,
its alternative codes of behavior, its equivocal values.
Intermingled with the desire is "the inchoate protest,
the sense of disenchantment; and the vague complaints
and forebodings that are already perceptible in the late
nineteenth-century art and literature have been diffused
into general consciousness. There they function as a kind
of vulgarized romanticism, a *Weltschmerz in per-
petuum,* a sickly sense of disturbance that is subter-
ranean but explosive." [10]

The various circumstances of discontent render the
individual especially receptive to suggestion. Significantly, this state of suggestibility may occur either when
the individual feels he knows the answers to his problems or when he is still groping for answers. The first
situation—in which the individual has a ready frame of
reference—has long been recognized. Words like "for-
eigner," "agitator," or "capitalist" may be trigger terms
which evoke in him automatic responses; these terms
identify, he believes, the sources of his problems. Less
attention has been given, however, to the situation in
which sheer bewilderment (rather than the "will to believe") is also conducive to suggestibility. [11] In this circumstance, the interpretation a person seeks may come
from a respected friend, a newspaper columnist, or the

leader of a social movement, but the degree of the individual's receptivity will depend on both the extent to which he lacks a frame of reference and the intensity of his desire for meaning.

Individuals in such situations are especially, though not uniquely, a product of the mass society. Whether sure of their own explanations and simply seeking ways to implement them or lacking explanations as well as means of solution, such individuals are vulnerable to the appeal of social movements: for movements provide both the answers and the promise of action.

A man of more than average initiative and impatience may attempt to form an organization that will meet his own difficulties and similar ones faced by others; or he may be one of the first to rally around such an effort. But if he is representative of the general population, he will wait for hardier souls to take the lead. He and others in a like state are a reservoir of unknown size upon which embryo movements draw for sustenance and growth. Their success in tapping that reservoir depends upon circumstances which will be explored in later chapters.

The Role of Modern Communication

The role played in social movements by modern communicative agencies can perhaps best be considered in terms of suggestibility since the effects of these agencies depends in large part upon the outlook and emotional state of the individuals whom they reach.

The press, radio, and television—and motion pictures to a lesser degree—clearly contribute to the bewilderment which may send the individual off in search of "meaning." Through these channels he is bombarded by ideas, standards, and information which would otherwise reach him in smaller quantities or not at all—given the size, mobility, and impersonal relationships of the mass society. Apart from the fantastic assortment of pleadings carried to him with every salvo of commercial advertising, opinions of every subgroup and agency which have access to channels of communication are also transmitted. Ideas and values—and they are many—can be displayed not only more rapidly and to more people than by face-to-face contacts but also with less personal or corporate responsibility for their implications and consequences.

In a different way, mass communications may stimulate the desire for meaning by intensifying the individual's awareness of the remote and impersonal forces at work beyond his horizon. International economic relations, political upheavals in distant places, wars and threats of war are brought into his living room with such persistency that he may well feel adrift in a world he can neither understand nor control.

While modern media of communication, through the sheer bulk and variety of their barrage, can create or heighten bewilderment, paradoxically they can also help to relieve the individual's sense of confusion. The radio and press convey answers to his questions, solutions to his problems. Experts, self-acclaimed authorities, and leaders of social movements are all within reach to explain th "real" basis of his troubles and to show the way out. If the individual already harbors vague notions about the cause of his ills, he now has the opportunity of selecting the expert or leader who is closest to his own position and who crystallizes everything into simple propositions, tidy arguments, and respectable solutions.

Modern mass communication has similar potentialities for the individual who is neither bewildered nor vague in his beliefs, the individual whose suggestibility stems from a rigid set of convictions and ideas previously acquired. He already "knows" the sources of his own problems and of the society in general. He is ripe for the leader or reformer who professes these convictions and apparently documents their validity. Since the individual in a mobile and heterogeneous society may be quite unaware of how many people beyond his personal observation share his convictions, mass communication is an instrument capable of revealing and building a far-flung camaraderie between unacquainted individuals seeking surcease from their discontent.

Modern media of communication, then, operate in several ways as a link between mass society and the growth of social movements. To be sure, not all media are crucial for a movement, and prior to 1920 or so only the press could play a significant role in any case. Their increasing importance is clear, however, and may be assumed for the future. They will probably continue to play the same dual role: enhancing the human desire for meaning by exposing individuals to the many and often confusing facets of the culture and subculture of their society; and at the same time airing a variety of "causes" and movements with interpretations and plans of action aimed at the bewildered and the opinionated alike.

Mass communications, thus, along with the confusions and dissatisfactions of modern life, are important for the general proliferation of social movements. The movements themselves, however, and the more specific circumstances of their growth and decline are the major concern of this study and will be the focus of the succeeding chapters.

2 The Nature of Social Movements

Movements, institutions, local events or episodes, and various kinds of organizations share certain characteristics. All four are marked by group activity, social relationships, and some sort of objective. Yet a movement such as Christian Science obviously does not belong in the same sociological category as a lynch mob, a family, or a college fraternity. A preliminary requirement, then, in the study of social movements is to distinguish them from groups and systems of association which they resemble.

Social movements, being dynamic, pass through several stages of development. Consequently their characteristics vary at different times. It may therefore be helpful to discuss the distinguishing features which are especially evident in the mature stage of any movement, when it is a "going concern."

Distinguishing Features of Social Movements

In the first place, social movements may be distinguished from other phenomena on the basis of the kind of goal to which they are committed. Unlike social institutions, their purpose is *change,* whether of relationships, norms, beliefs, or all of these. This does not mean that a given movement necessarily seeks to upset the entire social order or to convert all subgroups to its banner. But without some change in view there is no social movement. The alteration sought may be a specific piece of legislation or the realization of an abstract ideal. In either case it is a goal deliberately formulated and explicitly proclaimed. Occasionally a movement becomes petrified, disclaiming any such promise and appearing as a defender of the status quo. When this occurs, it is no longer a social movement but one of many agencies and organizations that function to promote some degree of social stability.

Secondly, movements employ *organization* as a means of achieving their goals. Sometimes they are organized from the very start, but in any event membership ties inevitably become formalized to some extent. In contrast with crowds and mobs, movements usually involve, for example, dues or other payments, record-keeping, explicit acceptance of a creed, and initiatory rituals. Membership in movements is colored by status distinctions between followers and functionaries, the latter being further specialized on the basis of difference in powers, responsibilities, and prestige. Frequently, there is one leader supreme both in prerogatives and in the dynamic qualities of his personality. His greatness may lie chiefly in oratory, administrative skill, or in his vision and insight, but it is there, casting across the multitude a shadow longer than that of lesser men.

Third, movements may be identified by their *geographical scope*. They differ from a factory strike or a local "citizens' reform movement" in extending beyond any single community. Though they start in some one place, movements soon break their local bonds. The number of local units or chapters reflects the broad purposes shared by all members, regardless of what local issues may confront them. Whether its scope be national, regional, or international, a mature movement transcends the local community.

Each of these three features, to be sure, characterizes many associations and agencies, but the convergence of all three is the distinctive mark of social movements. *Persistence through time* might be added as a fourth trait were it not for the problem of fixing some minimum duration. Some movements, such as Christian Science, are a long time maturing while others, such as the first Ku Klux Klan, develop and die within a few years. Nevertheless, there is a degree of durability not found in audiences and other transitory collections of people. Probably the factors of organization and extensive scope greatly help a movement to survive and to evolve into something more than an "episodic event." [1]

Definitions and Types of Social Movements

The social movement has been defined as a "collective ready for action by which some kind of change is to be achieved, some innovation to be made, or some previous condition to be restored" and as a "collective enterprise to establish a new order of life." [2] Both definitions emphasize the group and change-making aspects, and these features are certainly basic. But the organization and scope are also important. Throughout this study, then, a social movement will be understood to be *a group venture extending beyond a local community or a single event and involving a systematic effort to inaugurate changes in thought, behavior, and social relationships.*

The definitions above are broad enough to include several types of movements. Taking the objective of change as a starting point, varying degrees of change may be sought; some movements aim at a complete alteration of the social order, others at modifying only certain parts of it. The former have been classified as *revolutionary* and the latter as *reform* types of movements. Reform movements tend to stress existing ethics, are therefore considered more or less "respectable," and utilize discussion in gaining the support or tolerance of public opinion. Revolutionary movements, on the other hand, often attack traditional ethical codes, are so lacking in respectability that they are frequently driven underground, and seek converts rather than public commendation.[3] This dichotomy should not obscure the reality of a continuum between the two ideal types.

Organization too is a matter of degree. Movements that combine fraternal interests with more ambitious goals usually stand near one extreme: the hierarchy of offices is clearcut, "degrees" are obtained by the more aspiring members, numerous titles are bestowed, rituals tend to be complicated, and financial and other policy matters follow well-defined rules. At the other extreme are movements with only a skeletal organization: functionaries are few and are thought of as leaders rather than officials; ritual is simple or non-existent (though some expression of belief is invariably required of members, who are also called upon for material contributions). Organization is thus a "more-or-less" characteristic. However, patterns of behavior whose followers have no organization whatsoever—as in the case of fads in dress and the like—are not, according to the definition adopted here, social movements.

A third basis for distinguishing types of movements is *coordination*. Here the distinctions are sharper, though a few cases, such as the birth control movement, defy an either-or classification. Coordination may be regarded as a frequent and special function of organization: units or "chapters" are related not only by a common goal but by their concerted action to promote that goal. Since movements extend beyond the local community, they are composed of more than one, and usually numerous, local units. Each of these is itself organized to some degree, but each is also affiliated with others in a large overall structure. The latter may be regional, national, or even international in scope, and through it the separate units function in concordance. Although complete uniformity or consensus is never achieved, enough conformity with respect to policies and procedures exists so that the movement may be regarded as coordinated. Policies may be formulated at the top on the basis of proposals which flow upward through the member units; on the other hand, they may be designated in an authoritarian manner by a leader or functionary in movements where the units are merely dependent parts of a highly centralized structure. In either case, however, an announcement of policy is usually the signal for automatic compliance on pain of expulsion or loss of affiliation.

An uncoordinated movement, such as the "labor movement," operates without such an accord or all-embracing structure, but the several organized units share common goals and a similar body of doctrine. They are autonomous because they possess no formal structural ties with each other and lack any functioning agreement on tactics and specific policies. Should such uncoordinated units and activities be considered social movements at all? Common usage has established them firmly within the concept, and their greater resemblance to coordinated movements than to other social phenomena justifies their inclusion.[4] Neither coordinated nor uncoordinated movements should, quite obviously, be confused with the historical trends of which movements are one manifestation, whether as agent or consequence. A distinction must be made, for example, between industrialism and the labor movement or between a declining birth rate and the birth control movement.

Revolutionary movements are not treated in the present study, for revolution is a highly complex form of social change requiring a more detailed analysis than is possible here. The movements used as illustrations, then, are all of the reform type and provide examples of various degrees of coordination and organization.

Elements of Social Movements: Goals and Means

Goals The goal of any movement is the objective toward which the movement's activities are directed. Some form of social change is always *explicitly* indicated in that objective. Many movements are also oriented toward ends which are *implicit* rather than expressed, ends about which the participants may be aware only tacitly or about which they may be quite ignorant. Certain objectives may be nurtured by leaders who hope for great personal power and prestige, whether or not they sincerely believe in the explicit aims embraced by their followers; in other cases, the secrecy maintained by functionaries simply reflects their fear that the participants are not yet "ready" for, or will be alienated by, these goals.[5]

Besides their degree of explicitness, several other aspects of goals are observable. For one thing, a distinction may be made between *general* and *specific* goals. Most movements have both these kinds of objectives. General aims lend flexibility to organization and tactics;

being broad, they are likely to have wide appeal to potential members and sympathizers. Brotherhood, spiritual well-being, and prosperity, for example, are sufficiently abstract goals to permit various personal interpretations. On the other hand, a movement with only general goals may be hard put to maintain enthusiasm among its adherents or to distinguish itself effectively from movements with similar purposes. However broad some of the objectives, more specific and attainable goals are usually also formulated as appeals to special interests.[6]

Objectives may also be examined in the time dimension, that is, with respect to whether their attainment is sought in the immediate or in the distant future. Securing some favorable action from government—the primary wielder of power in the mass society—is an example of what may be called an *immediate* goal; another is enlargement of membership. Immediate goals are usually preliminary steps to *ultimate* goals, which are often the more abstract ideals of the movement.

Christian Science exemplifies the tendency of religious movements to embrace chiefly ends which are general and of long range. Lectures delivered by one of its early spokesmen reveal something of its ultimate purpose: the eradication of materialism, fear, and disease in the world through faith and knowledge. On the other hand, political and economic movements usually stress immediate goals, as did the Grange in its demands for improved economic conditions for the farmer through higher prices for his products and lower cost for his necessities.

A further dimension pertains to how substantial a change in the social order may be expected as a result of goal attainment. Revolutionary movements, of course, have as their ultimate aim a vital change in

large segments of the social order, whereas reform
movements pursue ends representing lesser social modi-
fications.[7]

While goals and the means for attaining them can be
separated for the purpose of analysis, objectives are
psychologically just as integral a part of any movement's operations as are its leaders or its rituals. As
emotional stimuli expressed in a movement's ideology,
they do constitute means in a limited sense. But seen
in the larger context of social change, they are also the
point toward which a movement is propelled, the end
toward which its efforts are directed. The means employed in this effort can be broken down into a variety
of categories which will here be limited to ideology,
group cohesion, organization, and tactics.

Ideology   More than merely stating its goals, the
ideology of a movement encompasses most of what is
essentially its culture. Whether written or unwritten, it
contains the justification for the movement's existence,
the values and ideals it cherishes, the rules by which
participants abide, and often some indication of the
sanctions behind those rules. Usually, too, there is a
negative doctrine stating what the movement is against.[9]
These negative issues may apply to specific groups and
organizations or, at times, to such abstractions as evil
and poverty. The ideology may be spelled out in detail
or represented in broad propositions which leave much
to inference and tacit understanding. In any event it is,
like a nation's constitution, the source from which a
movement derives its rationale, its doctrine, its course,
and its disciplinary principles.

In the case of Christian Science, positive norms and
values pertaining to man's relationships with his fellow-
men and with his God are revealed in the creed written

by Mrs. Eddy and subscribed to by the first members: "We solemnly promise to strive, watch, and pray for that Mind to be in us which was also in Christ Jesus. To love the brethren, and, up to our highest capacity, to be meek, merciful, and just, and live peaceably with all men." [10] An ideology of quite a different sort is employed by the Ku Klux Klan whose rationale centers around the dangers of race mixture and expresses repugnance for racial equality. While Klan leaders sometimes deny that the movement is against any specific racial or religious group, Klan actions and literature stamp it unambiguously as anti-Negro, anti-Semitic, and anti-Catholic.

Group Cohesion   A sense of loyalty and consciousness of kind are essentials for holding a movement together. The cement which makes cohesion possible may be composed of such ingredients as dedication to common aims and values, benefits incidental to the major objectives, negative sanctions, and inspirational leadership. But cohesion, whatever its primary source, is the element that gives a movement durability. When enthusiasm gives way to disenchantment, when the dedicated become the disaffected, the movement is headed for obscurity. Beyond simply retaining a membership, however, there is the problem of retaining a close-knit membership which can function effectively toward immediate or ultimate goals. Once disagreement gains momentum it can become an avalanche of dissension, leaving only broken fragments where there was once a united body. Although Moral Rearmament, for example, has experienced severe criticism and setbacks since its genesis, the movement continues to display a stubborn survival ability and cohesiveness. Chiefly responsible probably is its leader, Frank Buchman; but cohesion has also been generated through the members' enthusiastic and explicit dedication to the "Standards of Christ" and through the frequent meetings of small groups in which confessions—and thus guilts—are shared with others.

Organization and Status System The patterns of relationship between groups and statuses within a movement comprise, respectively, its organization and its status system. These are recognized by members though not all the details may be understood by them. The most obvious aspect of the patterns is the status distinction between leaders and followers and the roles played by each. Easily identified too is the difference in coordinated movements between local units and the overall organization of which they are a part and which operates through a central headquarters. Among the functionaries, status distinctions and definitions of roles may be more subtle and may elude ordinary members and outside observers. This obscurity of statuses is especially true when the real power is held by a minor functionary or someone who lacks a formal title, when a top office-holder is a mere figurehead manipulated by individuals whose formal status is relatively low. In social movements, as elsewhere, there are those who prefer power to public acclaim. There are also those who seem indifferent to both, perhaps securing their greatest satisfaction from a sheer sense of accomplishment.

Quite apart from the personal gains and motives involved, any group effort requires some division of labor. Special responsibilities and obligations must be assigned along with special rights and powers. More than that, if there is to be cooperative effort (that is, if anything is to get done), the relationships between specialized individuals and groups must somehow be defined. Undifferentiated cohesion is not enough, nor is mere agreement on goals. The sustained activities which bring results require an orderly social machinery. Individuals enter and leave, membership turnover may be slight or great, leaders come and go, but the system of statuses remains.

Of the various elements comprising a movement's status system, leadership carries the greatest potentialities for drama. But because the dynamic leader commands so much attention and often, in memory, outlives his cause, observers and members alike are prone to think of leadership largely in terms of drama and individual personality. Actually leadership is of many shades, and one useful distinction is that between charismatic and legal leaders.[11] The control exercised by the legal type derives from the office rather than from the man and his personality. His authority is legal or at least formal; it is usually defined in such ideological documents as constitutions and bylaws. His personal qualities may be ordinary or unusual, but it is by virtue of his office rather than these qualities that he claims obedience and deference. Oliver Kelley, founder of the Grange, well exemplifies the legal leader. While there is no question of his dedication to the movement and his selfless labors on its behalf, his prestige and authority derived chiefly from his having originated the idea of the Grange and from the office which he held; what moderate success he had in securing members was a product of his dogged persistence, not of his unremarkable personality.

The charismatic leader is of a different sort. He cannot be ordinary. The authority and powers he possesses are truly his, stemming from unique virtues which set him apart from others and above any formally defined status. Often he is the movement's founder as well as its supreme leader. Often, too, his power is very close to absolute, whatever appearance he may affect of "bowing to the will of the people." The status of lesser functionaries is linked to the charismatic leader in that they can be arbitrarily assigned powers by him. Close friends and loyal disciples may be given high-ranking positions—so long as they do not show signs of excessive ambition.

Even in a whole society, to say nothing of a social movement, there is rarely a new charismatic leader available when the old one dies or steps down. The legal leader then enters to replace him who led "by grace." Or the replacement may be by a small group, a form of executive committee. The authority of subordinate functionaries is no longer endowed by the leader but is defined in terms of the offices held. Skills and knowledge rather than personal ties govern appointments, and the movement is on its way to being bureaucratized.

Cautions about contrasting types representing only abstract poles (between which actual cases fall) are as applicable to leadership as to other matters. Probably no leader is all charismatic or all legal. But in the person of a Father Divine is found about as close a resemblance to the charismatic type as most mortals could aspire to. If his power is not absolute, it is very nearly so; if his personality has not molded the entire movement, the marks it has left are prominent and distinctive. His identification as God and his followers' belief in his physical immortality are added evidence of the charisma which resides in him.

Tactics Those activities and policies of a movement which are directed at the "outside world" are its tactics. They do not pertain to disciplining members or altering structural or ideological elements. They are, rather, the means by which attainment of goals is directly attempted and by which new members are ultimately brought into the fold. The same activity may, of course, serve both these purposes, but often dfferent techniques are required for each.

A catalog of all the tactics employed by social movements would be almost endless. In proselyting and in striving for goal-attainment, movements have drawn on virtually every method known to other agencies and organizations. Occasionally the techniques have been combined with originality; the component devices, however, are invariably borrowed rather than original.

Tactics are clearly dependent upon other elements within the movement. The suitability of this or that approach in terms of audacity or cautiousness, for example, varies with the size and cohesion of the membership, with the structure of the movement, and especially with the kind of leadership at hand. Ideology too is an influence for it may so exalt and justify the goals that almost any tactical devices seem excusable. The goals themselves are also a factor, ultimate ends calling for quite a different tack than more immediate aims. Always present as another condition of tactics is the social order as a whole. Violence, for instance, may seem appropriate for achieving some particular goal, but it is risky in the modern state which rarely tolerates the use of force by any but its own agencies.

Tactical blunders can be fatal to a movement. Errors —such as a show of weakness or, conversely, an ill-timed display of aggression—can alienate potential supporters and even members, however enthusiastic they may be about the goals. It is then that the integrity of leaders may be impugned and suspicions voiced about unrevealed goals, for the methods men employ are as much a product of their motives as are the ends which they profess. The Birth Control movement in the United States affords a good example of how diversified tactics can be, for among the devices it employed during its formative years were soap-box speeches, mass meetings, street-corner distribution of leaflets, mailed literature, books, legislative lobbying, court actions, and even letter-writing by a thousand-member committee. Margaret Sanger, the leader and founder of the movement in this country, early decided that the four main techniques should be "agitation, education, organization, and legislation." [12]

3 Careers of Social Movements

Social movements and their goals represent, respectively, actual and potential social changes. How social changes originate is an important problem; as important, however, is the question of what happens to an innovation after it has appeared. Therefore, to be socially realistic, analysis of social changes should include the phases or steps through which they pass. A novelty does not gain even limited acceptance at once, though the contrary is the belief of people who suddenly become conscious of a change which has long been incubating beyond their range of observation. In short, change is a process; it proceeds, sometimes slowly and sometimes rapidly, but there is always a graduation. The necessity of viewing change as a process is imposed not only by social realities but by limitations of human intellect and perception. Given the rather nebulous state of knowledge regarding social change, it is especially advisable to break the process down into manageable units, just as the novice musician must deal with each measure in turn rather than attempting to take in an entire page at a glance.

The career or "natural history" of a social movement may be viewed as a series of steps or a progression of phases. These may be seen in different ways: for example, on the basis of size of membership or degrees of advancement toward goals. One scheme often used embraces four stages: social unrest, popular, formal

organization, and institutionalization.[1] Such schematic
presentations serve both to stress the fact that movements undergo change and to suggest the nature and
direction of this change. In the descriptions which follow, a less comprehensive scheme is used in order to
distinguish and deal separately with two dimensions of
the career of every movement. The first dimension
pertains to successive internal alterations, that is,
events within the movement itself. The second dimension involves trends in the relations of the movement
with the external society, especially reactions of outsiders to the movement and its impact on various
groups and cultures. While these two dimensions are
interrelated in actual cases, they may be treated separately for purposes of analysis. Moreover, a given
stage of one dimension need not necessarily coincide
with a particular stage in the other. And the usual
word of caution is in order: the stages here described
are ideal types whose attributes are seldom fully
realized in a concrete movement.

Internal Development

Earlier, in discussing the characteristics of the mass
society, it was pointed out that while movements are
not unique to industrial and urban societies, such societies do provide a fertile soil for the germination and
growth of social movements. In this setting social
heterogeneity, cultural confusion, and mass communications often stimulate personal discontent which may
become manifest as social unrest. Such unrest, however, is less a stage in the career of a movement than
an essential background condition for its inception.

Inspection of the internal development of social
movements indicates that characteristically they are

marked by an incipient phase, an organizational phase, and a stable phase.

Incipient Phase   There is no reliable way as yet to predict whether a specific undertaking will eventually develop into a full-blown social movement. At the time of inception, most such undertakings are almost formless and frequently confused in purpose. Many show little promise of growth, sometimes because they have only local appeal or because their goals are so immediate and specific. Others show greater likelihood of evolving into movements because of the potentially wide appeal of their aims, the capacities of the founders, or the social and psychological needs which they meet. The difficulty in prediction stems largely from the dynamic nature of movements and their goals. Thus an incipient undertaking whose ends indicate the least likelihood of sustaining a genuine movement may nevertheless flourish because these ends are altered from time to time—or what seems a beginning with real promise may abort because a more effective organization with similar purposes appears on the scene. This is to say that "independent variables" are a potential source of embarrassment for the person who forecasts that this or that sign of social ferment is a movement in the making.

But the fact that the careers of social movements cannot be projected into the future with assurance does not rule out the value of tracing backward the growth of those movements which have reached or are reaching maturity. Stalking the game from its tracks to discover the direction it has taken often helps the hunter to anticipate the direction the quarry will take. This problem of prediction, of course, harasses the student of other manifestations of social change.

The incipient phase, then, is one which is only recognized and defined in retrospect. It begins when the individual or individuals chiefly responsible for the inception of a movement become conscious of this possibility. The point of origin, however, is less important than the immediate social consequences of the innovator's inspiration. The initial period extends through the time when a small nucleus of followers comes to share the leader's ideas and enthusiasm. Throughout this period, the organization of the movement is almost always simple (though its elaboration may already be envisaged by some members). Initial members necessarily constitute a primary group marked by face-to-face informal relationships, and generally there is no more differentiation of statuses than the inevitable distinction between the founder and his coterie. Refined status differences rarely emerge at this early stage. The beginnings of Christian Science exemplify well the rather nebulous quality of the incipient phase. Though some of the early disciples were held in greater esteem than others by both Mrs. Eddy and their associates, statuses were fluid and ill-defined among the followers. Tactics remained relatively unformulated; about the only goal explicitly recognized was the spreading of the Christian Science gospel and the conversion of outsiders to the faith.

Although some writers claim that the birth of a movement is necessarily attended by a charismatic leader (and his talents are undoubtedly helpful), cases can be found where, despite the absence of such leaders, movements have entered the world quite successfully. Contrariwise, his presence is no guarantee of success. The fact is that movements have been born through the efforts of some very ordinary people whose qualifications for leadership seem to have been chiefly enthusiasm and industry. Such a person was mentioned earlier: Oliver Kelley, founder of the Granger Movement and as unlike a charismatic leader as could be found. Indeed, when the national offices of the Grange were decided upon, he assumed the secretaryship rather than the presidency. Tireless and self-sacrificing though his efforts were, there is no evidence that he was a dominant policy-maker or in any way occupied a charismatic status.

During this first phase, goals are likely to be general and regarded by at least some members as immediately attainable; other ideological elements remain nebulous and tactics crude or unformulated. Loyalty is usually intense and group cohesion strong, re-enforced by personal contacts between founder and disciples and by the emotional momentum generated through participation in a new undertaking. The magnetic founder of the American movement for birth control, Margaret Sanger, describes her early cohorts in this way: "When they remained they found work, work, work, and little recognition, reward, or gratitude. Those who desired honor or recompense, or who measured their interest by this yardstick are no longer here." [2] At the same time, intimacy can also give rise to conflicts, and internal dissension is as possible now as in later stages. Limited size, experience, and resources make for vulnerability to opposing or competing groups. These and other hazards are especially formidable during incipience; hence a high mortality rate for young movements.

Organizational Phase   As the plans and ideas which originally existed only on paper or in the minds of founder and followers develop into systematic activities and a more definite organization, the movement enters its second phase. The transition takes place gradually, one phase blending into the next.

Organization becomes more and more complex as division of labor is made more specific. Though they are often untrained and part-time amateurs, functionaries are increasingly specialized in their activities and their offices are dignified by distinctive titles. Through the process of shuffling and re-shuffling of statuses, the outline of a hierarchy begins to emerge.

With respect to leadership types, generalization should be as cautious as in the case of the incipient phase. If the movement is founded by a charismatic leader, he may continue to head it throughout the organizational stage too. On the other hand, leadership may have evolved to the legal type. Elaboration of the hierarchy does not necessarily require a marked increase in the number of followers, for numerical growth may occur chiefly after such elaboration. The appearance of branches or chapters, however, as excrescences of the original group must wait upon membership expansion sufficient to support them. If the movement is a coordinated one, channels of communication and control are simultaneously developed to connect the local units with the central headquarters and perhaps with each other. The informality of the incipient stage is thus gradually lost, except among the local rank-and-file members. The Ku Klux Klan, for instance, achieved organization more rapidly than do most movements. The little group of Confederate veterans who founded it improvised much of the bizarre regalia and the equally bizarre offices which became the trademarks of the Klan. Soon the Southern countryside was flecked with white-robed, hooded night riders led by their Grand Dragons, Titans and Cyclops. With rapid growth in membership, state, county and community units appeared very early, all federated within an "Invisible Empire" which encompassed the entire South.

Ideological elements as well as structure undergo modification and rearrangement during the organizational phase. For example, in those movements where ceremony is emphasized, rituals will now be well worked out if they were not blueprinted previously; rarely are they developed or radically altered later on. Original goals are reappraised: some are now defined as ultimate rather than immediate possibilities, others discarded altogether in favor of quite different objectives. Since values and goals from the incipient phase are mainly of a general kind, they are now supplemented by more specific aims and values—especially if efforts at conversion have not been fruitful. The movement called Moral Rearmament illustrates this process of modification, for its original and rather nebulous goals of absolute purity, honesty, love and unselfishness were eventually overshadowed by emphasis on such objectives as industrial peace in the domestic sphere and pacifism in international relations.

Often neglected during the first phase, norms for behavior now become specified and so too their supporting sanctions. Proselytive tactics frequently change as trial and error proves some to be more effective than others; gradually they become more systematic and less a matter of improvisation or whim. Tactics of agitation are changed for the same reason and also for the sake of conforming with alterations in ultimate and immediate goals. Clearly, this stage of development is not only organizational but reorganizational as well.

In the organizational stage, a movement remains vulnerable to both external and internal threats to its survival. By altering goals and tactics with an eye to combating opponents or competitors, external hazards may be overcome. But the very steps necessary for success in that direction may at the same time alienate the faithful or create internal dissension. Rapid growth at this stage carries inherent dangers as new members bring into the movement new points of view; the reservoir of potential functionaries swells and competition for status achievement is intensified; local units may seek greater autonomy and local leaders greater recognition; the apostate becomes an increasing possibility and with him a major internal cleavage. Then too, many who join under impulse, in a flush of enthusiasm, may easily become disenchanted—especially if immediate satisfactions are not strong or if there is scant evidence of progress toward the attainment of goals.[3] The Birth Control movement in the United States experienced these growing pains in the 1920's when internal differences of opinion arose over financial policies, the recruitment of members, and the role of birth-control clinics; consequently the founder and the Birth Control League she had helped build went separate ways, each to make a new beginning.

Stable Phase The organizational phase does not persist indefinitely in long-lived movements (although no undertaking can evolve into a full-fledged social movement without first attaining this stage). Any venture remaining in an extreme state of ferment dissipates its energies, so to speak, to the point of exhaustion: hence, some degree of stabilization is eventually required.

Another reason for stabilization is that, as noted earlier, movements are one refuge for those members of a mass society who are in search of security, unequivocal values, and definite—even dogmatic—answers to their questions. The hope of finding meaning and direction for at least some part of their lives makes people converts. If, instead, normlessness and shifting goals are encountered, the hopeful convert may soon become a disgruntled deserter. Thus, some movements experience a high turnover in membership which can weaken group cohesion even though the total number of members does not decline.

These are some of the circumstances that guarantee that movements which persist beyond their days of organization and fermentation undergo a process of stabilization. Here stability does not refer either to the position of the movement in the greater society or to its numerical membership; it refers rather to an *internal* development during which the unsettled, organizational phase gives way to clarification and stabilization of the component elements of the movement. Goals are no longer shifting nor values transitory; tactics and other activities, no longer hit or miss, are now prescribed. Perspiration replaces inspiration as the basis of accomplishment. This is not to equate stability with a static condition, for ossification can be as fatal as continued instability. But the movement must attain enough equilibrium so that people can perceive clearly its aspirations and how it plans to realize them. The Grange affords an interesting case of a movement which, in its stable phase, returned to some of the original goals it discarded during the process of organization; at the same time the militancy and radicalism of its organizational phase was sloughed off, and—apart from agricultural problems—the movement in recent decades has generally favored the status quo.

Organization, as well as ideology and tactics, becomes more clearcut and orderly. A charismatic leader may postpone or limit stabilization, but with the end of such leadership the stable phase becomes imminent and inevitable. Principles for selecting the topmost leader or functionary must be formulated; other positions of authority and prestige must be given an air of legitimacy; and this process of routinization involves "transition from a charismatic staff . . . to one which is adapted to everyday conditions." [4] For example, the death of Mary Baker Eddy left Christian Science relatively unshaken, for she had herself instituted a complex and effective bureaucracy—headed by a self-perpetuating board of directors—to carry on the movement which had acquired its original momentum at her hands.

Unlike the earlier phases, stabilization requires a distinctive type of leadership, the legal as contrasted with the charismatic. The relationship of this leadership type to ideological elements is clear: legal authority involves a belief in the "legality" of rules and the right of those elevated to authority under such rules to issue orders. Conformity is largely obedience to legal commands, to an impersonal order, and not to an exalted or adored individual. Offices are organized as a bureaucratic hierarchy, each under the supervision of another on a higher level. Administrative functionaries are usually appointed, though the top-level functionaries may hold office through election, designation, or even appropriation. The sphere and function of each office are clearly defined and the candidates are chosen presumably because they are technically qualified. Mere enthusiasm is not as sufficient an asset as it was in earlier stages. The officials are not bound to the legal chief as they were to the charismatic leader; they are personally free, apart from their impersonal official obligations. With such bureaucracy the performance of daily activities and operations can be routinized for maximum efficiency; internal stabilization of the movement as a whole is achieved.

External Development

The stages of internal development just described may not be applicable to phenomena other than social movements. But the kind of progression which movements show in the external aspects of their careers is characteristic of many innovations. The developmental stages indicated here are broad rather than incisive. Their purpose with respect to change in general and movements in particular is chiefly to reveal the gradualness with which new elements achieve acceptance in a society. They also serve as reminders of the complexity of social change (without any pretense that they provide answers to the questions evoked by this complexity). Lastly, some series must be adopted in order to discuss changing relationships between the movement and the greater society in which it occurs, in appraising its success, or even in determining what "success" implies.

The three phases to be referred to here are: innovation, selection, and integration. Each term is descriptive of both a phase in the graduated career of any movement and a process which the movement is undergoing at that time.

The questions being raised in this section, then, pertain to what happens to the movement rather than what happens to the society as a consequence of the existence and activities of the movement. And the terms innovation, selection, and integration here pertain only to the external career of movements in the greater society.

One additional complication which must be noted is that social acceptance is a problem involving two elements: the movement itself and the changes which it strives to bring about. From the observer's point of view, the movement as such is an agency or means, distinguishable from the goals toward which it is oriented. Each constitutes a social change. Hence, both movements and the goals they underwrite are subject to similar processes and similar degrees of acceptance with reference to the society in which they occur. If successful, both are accepted first by a very few individuals, then by increasing numbers until they become incorporated by numerous subgroups and perhaps ultimately by the society as a whole. But in terms of acceptance, the movement and its goals may proceed separately, one more rapidly than the other, one failing to achieve a degree of acceptance which the other attains. Some movements have lost ground or even failed to survive while one or more of their goals has been widely looked upon with favor. The movement rather than its goals will be central to the discussion that follows.

Innovation   The act or process of introducing a new element into a society is called innovation, and the element itself often termed an innovation. The element may be "any thought, behavior, or thing that is new because it is qualitatively different from existing forms." [5] Innovation is, of course, the source and beginning of all social changes. Itself a complex process, it has been a point of interest for sociologists and especially for anthropologists who have long carried on a debate regarding the comparative importance of diffusion and invention as innovative processes. The chief concern here, however, is with the general career of innovations rather than their "causes" or the circumstances of their genesis. The question is not so much how they get started as what happens after they appear. In terms of the latter problem the most interesting and significant trait of innovations is their high mortality rate. In a mass society, social novelties are spawned with a profusion and persistence that rivals the oyster's remarkable performance on the biological level. Casual observation (as well as patent-office statistics) reveals the abundance of material inventions, but non-material variations also appear in staggering numbers. To take one of the most impressive examples, the utopias of which men have dreamed and still dream fill an increasing number of shelves in our modern libraries. But in the whole range of new elements—from perpetual-motion machines to brave new worlds—only a tiny proportion survive beyond the process of innovation. Although conceived and displayed for examination, most novelties are never adopted. Indeed the cultural past of any society is, for the most part, a vast graveyard occupied by the innovations which died with their authors.

While the *process* of innovation is a characteristic of all societies, a given innovation cannot technically be considered part of a culture. By definition it is novel, not normative. Seen in its social setting, it is a peculiarity of the inventor or of the very small group which initially sponsors it. Without some spread in popularity, its life span must be short and its ultimate fate must be social oblivion, an object of interest for the antiquarian.

Selection Important though the innovator is in social change, there has been a tendency to inflate his stature beyond realistic proportions. As a result the shadow he casts has grown to such magnitude as to obscure two other agents involved in change. Just as significant as the inventor are the proponent and the opponent of his innovation. Once a new item has been conceived, its ultimate place in the social order depends less on its originator than on those to whom it is displayed. The crucial roles of the proponent and opponent should be recognized and examined together with the selective process in which they participate.

The term selection is here used broadly to cover the processes of both the social acceptance and the rejection of innovations.[6] The direction that selection takes in society determines, as in the biological world, which items will survive as relatively permanent features of the social order and which will be eliminated. If selected out, rejected, an innovation remains peculiar to its author and has little social significance—though occasionally such ideas or inventions are resurrected by a later generation and then widely adopted. The period during which selection occurs is thus a testing period. Having once been introduced, a novelty is on trial, and its ultimate fate is determined by the reactions of people other than the innovator. The process of selection is often a long and drawn-out affair, some members of the society accepting the new proposal readily, others remaining apathetic or opposed. Federal price support for American farmers has been such a case. Sometimes rejection on all sides is immediate: for example, the fate of George Bernard Shaw's proposal that England become polygamous after the first World War.

Neither the direction the selective process will take nor the length of time it will continue can be predicted with confidence. Many factors are involved—some of them lying within the movement itself, others outside it —whose influence will be discussed later, but one point should be stressed here: any estimate of the success of a movement must be made with the distinction in mind between the movement as an organization and the goals toward which it is oriented. Each is subject to selection. When both are simultaneously accepted or rejected, estimating the degree of success of the movement is relatively easy. Such appraisals are seriously complicated, however, when goals find wide social acceptance while the movement as a whole enjoys little popularity.

The sheer emergence of a movement constitutes, after all, a social innovation: the structure, ideology, and tactics combined as they are in a particular way add up to something new on the social scene. On the other hand, the venture always exists for a purpose, an objective which also amounts to an innovation. In some instances, attainment of this objective robs the movement of its reason for existence and results in its collapse, as happened to the abolitionists after Emancipation. In other instances, a movement persists although its original goals find scant acceptance and are replaced by new ones. As noted earlier, the emphasis of Moral Rearmament on pacifism in the late 1930's was then a new development, soon to be undercut by the eruption of World War II. Yet the movement has persisted, and since the war the traditionally dominant ideals of pacifism and world brotherhood have been displaced by militance and aggression in an anti-Communist crusade. Not only may goals be selected independently of other elements in a movement (and certain goals accepted while others are rejected), but when acceptance of any element does occur it may—

as the students of diffusion have long since pointed out—acquire new meanings or new functions other than those intended by the originator.

Acceptance, then, is a matter of degree in two respects: a movement and all its goals may not be socially acceptable as a complete package since some items are separable and fare differently in the selective process; furthermore, when it does occur, acceptance rarely involves the entire society but usually means that only certain individuals or subgroups within the society are favorable in their reactions.

While the extended survival of a social movement is impossible without fairly wide acceptance, such acceptance by no means guarantees survival. Some movements have lost favor almost overnight with the very population segments which were once receptive and enthusiastic. Some movements of restricted scope have, on the other hand, grown almost imperceptibly, remained virtually dormant for a time, and then found acceptance in new quarters. Such mixed and vacillating reactions in the society indicate that the process of selection is continuing, that the ultimate outcome is still in doubt; either total rejection or relatively permanent integration are possible.

A chronological summary of the career of the Grange shows how erratic the process of selection can be. During the first two or three years after its inception, the movement found little acceptance in rural America. Its rapidly increasing popularity thereafter is revealed by the existence of 1150 local chapters by the fifth year of its existence, 7255 by the sixth year and 21,697 by the seventh year. In the seventh year 1875, a peak of about three quarters of a million members and one million supporters was reached. Since there were then only about three and a half million farms in the United States, it is clear that a remarkably large portion of the farming population had finally either accepted the movement itself or at least were supporting its activities and were sympathetic to its goals. But then the Grange skidded to a standstill; it not only ceased growing but began losing its members almost as quickly as it had acquired them. By 1889, all but a hundred thousand had deserted. The loss was checked at that point and slowly membership was rebuilt, though this time four plodding decades were required to secure the same numerical acceptance previously achieved in seven years.

Integration Like selection, integration as a process is little understood. Its consequences can be more readily described than can the means or steps by which they come about. When an innovation has found continuing social acceptance and thus passed the test of selection, the last phase of its career may be best described as integrative. Integration does not, however, imply absolute permanence of the item involved; taking the long-range view, truly permanent elements in any society are as scarce as the proverbial hen's teeth. Neither does integration imply universality. Rarely accepted by an entire society, a novelty usually diffuses to only certain segments within the society. Its popularity may be limited to a single community, to an occupational category, or to a particular social class. In fact, the distinctiveness of many subgroups is itself a result of their having adopted innovations which the rest of the society has rejected—for instance, the Quakers and Prohibitionists. To say that an item which began as an innovation has ultimately become an integrated part of a society's way of life is merely to say that it has taken its place among the norms and traditions of the society. Favorable selection of a novelty does not guarantee eventual integration but is a necessary condition for integration.

The criteria by which integration may be identified are in part psychological. In the first place, an integrated element (in rare cases) may come to be regarded as traditional or as normative for an entire society. The incest taboo would exemplify this. Secondly (and more commonly), although society-wide adoption may be lacking, the item acquires traditional and normative overtones at least for certain subgroups identifiable to most of the society's members. The members of a social movement which has attained social integration—as has Mormonism, for instance—would compose such a subgroup or "socially recognized category," and their practices and beliefs would be in the nature of cultural "specialties" which are not shared by the total population.[7] In other words, while most members of a mass society are not likely to belong to a given movement or share its cultural traits, they may nevertheless condone the movement and regard its practices and beliefs as customary for others. Then too, some statuses are so defined that their occupants are theoretically precluded from participating in certain movements (though exceptional cases of participation actually do occur): for a factory owner, however liberal, to join the labor movement or for a man, however sympathetic, to join a feminist movement would be socially contradictory and inappropriate.

From a sociological viewpoint, integration might best be defined functionally. That is, an integrated item is one which is tied in closely with other cultural elements and contributes to the existence or operation of the society. It is a working part of the social machinery and operates in conjunction with some of the other parts. For example, given the values and norms of American society, labor unions play an active part in industrial effectiveness and are linked to other functioning agencies through union-management committees and contracts, government arbitration boards, labor legislation, etc. And with respect to instilling and enforcing moral codes and maintaining a belief in supernatural sanctions, the function of diverse religious faiths in the United States is obvious—although the role of some of the smaller denominations in the society is still obscure.

By any of the above criteria it is apparent that few movements ever become a truly integrated part of a society although many are introduced as innovations. Because the selective process is therefore so important in the careers of movements and because it has been long neglected as an aspect of social change, it will be the focus of interest in the following chapters.

4 Selection and the Problem of Motives

The minimum requirement for the survival of a movement is membership. Since a full-blown movement extends beyond the local community, it must eventually embrace more than the small coterie characteristic of its incipient stage. For membership growth not only increases financial and human resources but also renders the movement more conspicuous and often more prestigeful—all of great tactical value in securing still more members and working toward professed objectives. The question to be considered in the remaining chapters is: what circumstances enable a movement to survive and flourish? *

Growth as an Index of Selection

There are several reasons for posing such a question. In the first place, the movement itself constitutes a social change of greater or lesser extent, depending on its size and activities. Its presence on the social landscape alters that landscape, and for certain segments

* The problem of a movement attaining its ultimate goals, why it fails or succeeds in changing relationships and behavior patterns in the greater society is a question of a different order and one which is beyond the scope of present analysis. It may be noted, however, that to exert such a maximum influence on a society's institutions, numerical growth is generally a prerequisite. Such growth is therefore not only an immediate objective of any movement, but also a preliminary criterion of its success as a movement.

of the population actions and attitudes are affected, even if their response is antagonistic and sporadic. Clearly, movements must be reckoned with by societies as a matter of expedience in formulating and enforcing policies, whether of a political, economic, religious, or moral nature. Christian Science, for example, has won over relatively few Americans to all the values and beliefs which it espouses, and it has yet to remove conflict in social relations or the kind of error which it claims lies at the basis of sin, pain, and anxiety. Nevertheless it has apparently become a permanent religious denomination and thus has altered the denominational structure of the nation. Too, its norms tabooing certain medical practices result in social ramifications which must be taken into account by the local community. Secondly, the growth of a movement calls for examination because it serves as the best available index of its success in diffusing the beliefs which it espouses, including belief in the importance of its ultimate goals. An increase in the number of converts is by no means a perfect index but is the most reliable clue available to this process of acceptance of ends.

Extending membership involves, however, more than goal acceptance. Where any action is entertained by human beings, a problem arises concerning the means to be employed in reaching the objective. Therefore, membership growth can be regarded as a rough indication that the joiners not only accept the goals of the movement as their own but also accept its tactics and structure as means to those goals. At any given time, of course, there are probably people in the society who believe in the desirability of the goals toward which a given movement is oriented but who never join because they view the means employed as inexpedient or unethical or both.

While it would be technically correct to assume that some part is played in selection by every element of a movement and by each of its individual members and that virtually every item of the external setting also constitutes a determinant, appraising the relative influence of all related factors and persons would be an obviously impossible task. The scope of the following chapters is therefore limited to making explicit the relevance of the component parts of movements to acceptance or rejection. In addition, some of the more evident aspects of the social setting will be searched out for the same purpose.

Motives and the Acceptance of Innovations

Before pursuing further the main theme of sociological factors in selection, a brief digression is called for to point up several psychological aspects of the selective process, to reconsider the condition referred to earlier as social unrest, and to relate it more specifically to the selection of social movements viewed individually rather than as general phenomena. For despite the turbulence and unrest which characterize mass societies, only a minority in these societies become members of social movements. Furthermore, those who do join a movement enter it with degrees of enthusiasm which vary with their motivation.

The nature and strength of motives leading an individual to accept or reject any innovation are not always clear to the person himself. They certainly are not self-evident to the observer, for real motives may be deliberately or unconsciously concealed. In any event, their inherent complexity makes conclusive appraisals of them difficult. On the other hand, a few general observations can be made regarding the types of individuals who are receptive to new proposals and are thus potential members of movements.

Biographical Determinants In addition to the nature of particular proposals and the conditions under which they are made, an individual's general receptiveness to innovations is a product of biographical factors: experiences, events, and relationships of his life history promote a dissatisfaction with certain customs or values of his society. This dissatisfaction represents a constellation of attitudes which are *antecedent* to the proposals he regards with favor.[1] To suggest that there are such generally receptive individuals is simply to say that the category of concern at the moment would fall near the "acceptance" end of an acceptance-rejection range.

Information on the relative importance of biographical determinants making for receptivity to change would be invaluable in many ways, especially in predicting the growth of various kinds of movements. In its absence, the general importance of these determinants can at least be recognized. One author has offered a classification of four types of individuals who are potential acceptors of innovations: (1) the dissident—people who, though perhaps conventional in their overt behavior, consistently object to some conventions of their group; (2) the indifferent—those who are not necessarily critical of conventions but are not dedicated to them; (3) the disaffected—those who are critical at the moment of conventions they formerly supported; they may vacillate between accepting the new or retaining the old, depending upon the situation; and

(4) the resentful—those who, not disinterestedly critical, comprise the envious have-nots who believe a change might benefit their circumstances and are therefore receptive to it.[2]

These four classes of potential acceptors are intended to describe fairly stable and identifiable categories existing at any time in societies, irrespective of specific proposals for change and the particular organizations or agencies advocating the proposals. Of course, the nature of the proposals and agencies supporting them may very well generate receptive attitudes in individuals who would not fall within the four categories. The point made here is simply that biographical determinants as well as the attributes of novelties are involved in the problem of motivation.

These biographical factors are themselves engendered by the complexities and confusions of the mass society. Many members of the mass society share certain biographical determinants because their position in the society is similar. That is, some of the experiences and relationships of virtually all Negroes or farmers or Protestants will have been similar. Because of this similarity of experience, an area of dissatisfaction exists which is common to and especially characteristic of a given subgroup. (Of course, there are additional areas which are shared by several subgroups.)

Also included in biographical determinants, however, are experiences which are in some respects unique to each individual. Some individuals, therefore, see their positions as more anomalous than others of similar status, for they have been swept by unpredictable forces into situations more bewildering and disconcerting than have their neighbors or friends.

The Role of Crisis Not all individuals, however, who might be classified as dissident, disaffected, indifferent, or resentful are impelled by their dissatisfactions to act in some drastic and deviant fashion. Before many of these potential acceptors of innovations are transformed into active ones, their discontent must be further intensified. And the intensity demanded for rebellious action is a product of what has been called *crisis*.[3] A crisis exists when an individual's life experiences have produced in him a state of chronic discontent and when his discontent is intensified by a convergence of events and forces in a single situation representing to him a culmination of his chronic dissatisfactions. Crisis provokes concrete action. The potential acceptor of a social change becomes an actual acceptor—often by joining a social movement.

Now some degree of dissatisfaction exists in all societies at all times. Complete interpretations or understanding of the forces which make a people's destiny is never accessible to them. Probably no part of a social system is satisfying to all members of a society, and no member of a society is satisfied with every part of the system. Crisis, however, is a product not of mere dissatisfaction but of frustrations which are actively resented because they are regarded as unnecessary and avoidable, the consequence of unjust action or inaction by other groups or individuals.[4] Crisis involves, then, the element of deprivation, the elimination (or threatened elimination) of something the individual views as essential and feels he has the right to expect.[5] Social movements may be viewed as one device by which people try to secure those essentials they believe are due them. Movements as adjustive techniques seem especially inviting when a time or situation is critical, when the feeling is abroad that certain dissatisfactions are not an inevitable penalty of social living and can be reduced or removed by some action, especially group action.

One qualifying comment should be made regarding the nature of crisis. Most human needs and desires are culturally defined, a matter of societal or subgroup expectations. The feelings of frustration which result when these needs are not satisfied are therefore themselves partly a product of cultural definitions. Except for cases involving minimum biological requirements, crises—like the deprivations which generate them—are not absolute. Crises are usually relative to the expectations which the individual has acquired from his groups. A situation which appears critical to members of one subgroup might be taken in stride by members of another. One individual may be provoked to action by deprivations which another meets with indifference or which for him are not deprivations at all.

Members and Their Motives   Important though critical situations are to the acceptance or rejection of social movements, a further examination of motives suggests that there are also other significant influences on membership growth. True, most people who join a movement do so subscribing to its ideology and its goals which they view as an answer to some crisis; individuals of this type are motivated by the belief that they will somehow benefit by the social changes to be effected when the movement attains its objectives. This largest group may therefore be called *goal-oriented*. (Of course, it is not homogeneous, for some individuals who are goal-oriented are fanatics, some merely enthusiasts, and still others enter the movement with strong mental reservations.)

Another and much smaller group of individuals, the *utilitarian,* seeks immediate benefits quite unrelated to the professed goals. Some of these people, the most ambitious, may hope to manipulate and redirect the movement toward goals best known and most profitable to themselves. Others seek professional opportunities or merely jobs, viewing occupational opportunities in the same light as they would posts in a business firm or government agency. While specific motives here are no more uniform than in the case of goal-oriented members, the individuals share a common trait: the lack of conviction about or feeling of loyalty to the movement's goals, its ideals, or its ideology. A third and last group comprises people who resemble the utilitarians in that they enter the movement with motives unrelated to personal crisis. At the same time they also resemble the goal-oriented joiners in being dedicated to the movement's objectives. This is the *altruistic* group. Here are the extreme idealists, seeking nothing materialistic for themselves but deeply concerned with the welfare of others. The underlying motives of the altruist are baffling, perhaps even to himself. It may be that his activities on behalf of other people can be attributed to "an outraged sense of order, or economy and efficiency, or of beauty, not in regard to matters touching the immediate, much less the material, interests of the individual, but in regard to social maladjustments which offend the (otherwise comfortable) individual's sense of justice, fitness, and balance." [6] While the size of this group cannot easily be determined, it would seem that pure altruism is a very scarce commodity. Indeed, the altruistic and utilitarian groups combined probably include far fewer people than would be classified as ordinary or goal-oriented members. Yet their importance should not be discounted. Through the offices they occupy and through the talent and prestige they possess, their influence in a movement can be far greater than their numerical strength would suggest.

Classifying potential and actual members of movements and pointing out the role of crisis—none of this resolves the problem of motives in connection with social movements, nor does it even exhaust all the questions which might be raised. But one accomplishment may be to clear the air of popular notions that the appeal of movements is limited to neurotics and crackpots. More important, the preceding discussion underscores the complexity of the selective process and the impossibility of glibly forecasting the degree of acceptance a movement will enjoy. Furthermore, it should now be clear that a diversity of motives together with the element of crisis are universal conditions under which selection occurs; they are the minimum, constant factors involved in the acceptance of any movement regardless of its inherent characteristics or the values and structure of the external society. In the chapters which follow, these biographical and psychological factors will be largely taken for granted since the discussions will center around somewhat more tangible and accessible factors imbedded in movements themselves and in their social setting. Fortunately, sociological analysis "does not require a full knowledge of how every person views himself and his world from one day to the next. . . ."[7]

5 Internal Factors in Growth

The growth of any social movement is determined by both its internal composition and the external structural and cultural characteristics of the greater society of which it is a part. The distinction between *internal* and *external* factors of growth should not obscure the inevitable interconnections between them, which are to be found in the life histories of all concrete social movements. But this distinction is useful for analysis. Moreover, internal elements, including both goals and the various means employed in their pursuit, can be shown to influence the growth of social movements independently of external conditions in some measure. This is the theme of the present chapter in which, incidentally, is employed the same topical scheme found in Chapter Two.

Goals

Some individuals join a movement for reasons unrelated to its objectives; other people subscribe to these objectives but never join. Since goals do influence the decision of many persons to join or to ignore a movement, its proposals must be included among the factors determining its fate. Now the degree to which goals find favor in a population may be largely a consequence of their acceptability as defined by the existing culture—a problem discussed in the following chapter.

Another problem, however, is: what *intrinsic* qualities of the goals may influence acceptance and rejection? First of all, realism with respect to basic human needs is an obviously advantageous attribute. When relief from such organic tensions as those of sex, pain, or metabolism is ruled out by idealistic aims, the movement committed to those aims bears a serious handicap from the start. The same may be said of goals that stifle satisfactions which, though learned, are universal or nearly so: prestige and security, for example.

Secondly, as viewed by the individual, some goals have an apparent and perhaps even a demonstrable utility while others show little promise of bringing satisfactions and hence elicit little enthusiasm. The criterion of utility is especially significant among converts who have examined the goals in only cursory fashion, intrigued chiefly by their novelty. But when the new becomes commonplace, the question is soon raised by the former enthusiasts: can the objectives—if attained —produce the satisfactions claimed by their proponents? [1]

Third, a lack of flexibility (often characteristic of specific, immediate goals) can prove detrimental to the growth of a movement. Changing external conditions may strip inflexible goals of their relevance and appeal. General and even rather nebulous objectives permit more ready adjustment since they lend themselves to many and often radically different interpretations. Religious or other super-empirical objectives, on the other hand, sometimes benefit from a rigid definition that gives an impression of finality and stability and hence may be conducive to feelings of security for subscribers.

Fourth, there is the matter of apparent attainability —that is, attainability in the eyes of potential members rather than the objective observer. Even allowing for the occasional power of expert propaganda to make impossibly ambitious goals appear achievable, some movements—for example, certain types of anarchism—have set their sights above credibility. On the other hand, the Ku Klux Klan of the 1860's is a good example of a movement with quite plausible aims: the elimination of Negro voting and office-holding, the expulsion of Northern carpetbaggers, and the "protection" of Southern whites from racial equality.

The intrinsic attributes of goals represent the barest requirements for the growth of a movement. Goals possessing favorable attributes—those that are realistic, flexible, attainable, and possess utility—do not guarantee that a movement will be greeted with enthusiasm. But a movement whose goals lack these attributes does not have the minimum assets for success.

Means

While all the elements of a movement earlier classified as "means" exist so that some desired social change will be brought about, these elements also have a very real bearing on the fate of the movement itself as a social system. Inadequacies of one element can negate adequacies in another; and certain elements, such as tactics, are more directly related to a movement's growth than are others, such as ideology. Although a few general points can be made about the way each element functions or fails to function for a particular movement, the elements generally cannot be ranked according to greater or lesser importance.

Ideology   Since goals are incorporated in ideology, an ideology stands or falls with the goals it encompasses and from which it is largely derived. Values, attitudes, and norms justify and interpret goals; they also reinforce belief in goals and the need for action in their achievement. At the same time, the ideology defines (through norms) and justifies (through values) the kind of action and machinery necessary for the attainment of goals. In other words it deals not only with goals but with tactics and with such status problems as leadership. The minimum function of an ideology in a successful movement is to provide a rationale not only for the objectives but for the tactical and organizational means to those objectives—it must make a good case for what the movement is trying to do and how it is trying to do it.

Ideology seen in this light is distinguishable from propaganda only by a thin line, propaganda being a more blatant, specific, and simplified version of a movement's ideology. The content of propaganda is often transitory, modified from situation to situation for reasons of expedience: its guiding principle is opportunism. Ideology, on the other hand, is relatively stable, often codified as a body of tenets closely woven around the central ideas and ideals of the movement. Whereas propaganda is improvised, sometimes crudely, to suit a particular audience of potential converts, ideology contains the basic doctrine to which all members are expected to subscribe. On the one hand, ideology is the dogma deduced from goals and, on the other, it is a statement of justification for seeking them. Broadly speaking, ideology relates (more or less logically) the various elements of the movement into a pattern and also relates the movement to its social setting.

In contrast to propaganda, the contribution of ideology in winning converts is typically limited and indirect, its function being chiefly to unite and guide those who are already members. Nevertheless in its more erudite guises it adds a flavor of respectability and thus appeals to those thoughtful people whom obvious propaganda might not touch. Propaganda—with its emotionalism, exaggerations, and over-simplifications—often attracts those who view intellectual appeals with suspicion.

Organization and Status System In Chapter Two the status system and organization of a social movement were described as the structure of relationships between statuses and groups, respectively. The aspect of status within movements most commonly emphasized, often to the neglect of other elements, is leadership. This emphasis is understandable, for when a leader is of dynamic or dazzling personality he is likely to be viewed as the source from which the movement draws its energy and growth. Furthermore, leadership provides a simple explanation for the growth of social movements in the same way that the "great man" has proved an attractive basis for interpreting the course of history. But the careers of social movements, resembling the twists and turns of history, cannot be attributed to any single factor.

While a powerful individual at or near the head of a social movement can exert great influence upon its goals, tactics, and ideology, leadership is only one component of the status system of a movement; and no single leader is ever omnipotent. Therefore, rather than an analysis of leadership as such, the purpose here is to consider this element with relation to other features of social movements.

Minimal leadership competence is essential for the survival of a movement, to be sure, but even outstanding leadership is no guarantee of survival. Nor is a particular type of leadership, such as the charismatic, altogether essential for particular stages in the development of a movement. Rather, the type of leadership required at different stages is the consequence of a complex combination of many conditions, including, for example, the kind of goals, the nature of the opposition, and the degree of unrest in the society.

With respect to the broader aspects of status distinctions, a scheme which is relatively simple yet adequate for exploratory purposes divides members of movements into two categories: *personnel* and *functionaries*. The first consists of ordinary members whose participation is sporadic and whose roles are unspecialized. Functionaries, on the other hand, are the persistently active members whose roles are likely to be more specifically defined. Three types of functionaries may be identified: (1) the *leader:* the individual in the role of leader has also often played the role of founder (or successor to the founder), frequently appearing to outsiders and the personnel itself as responsible for the policies and objectives distinctive to the movement. In fact, his influence within the movement may be more apparent than real, and in rare instances this type of functionary may be altogether absent. (2) the *bureaucrat:* [2] whether his status is high or low, his activities are predominantly administrative. The high-ranking bureaucrat is a policymaker responsible for the efficient operation of the movement's internal machinery whereas his bureaucratic subordinates are concerned with routine paperwork and the details of carrying out the major decisions handed down from above. (3) the *agitator:* this type serves as a liaison between the movement and the outside world, his chief function being either promotion or proselyting. In the former instance the agitator's responsibility is to further directly the goals of the movement by publicity, propaganda, lobbying, legal sanction, or other suitable tactics. In the role of prose-lyter, the agitator is essentially a missionary whose objective is to convert outsiders into members.

Some movements develop specialized functionaries earlier in their careers than do others, but if a movement survives the organizational stage and achieves stability, a degree of differentiation between bureaucrats and agitators is almost inevitable. In the case of Christian Science, for instance, Mrs. Eddy played the role of a dramatic and influential leader. At the same time, she had the foresight to design a hierarchy of statuses for the nurture and guidance of the movement after her death. (Father Divine, incidentally, has apparently failed to make similar preparations, and it seems likely that his Peace Mission movement will dissolve when he dies—an event he and his most ardent followers refuse to consider possible.) Topmost in the Christian Science hierarchy is the Board of Directors which determines all officers of the central Mother Church in Boston. Besides controlling these and many other specialized bureaucrats throughout the movement, the Board's dominance over all classes of agitators is also complete: for example, it certifies healers and lecturers, it supervises both publication and—through the Board of Education—teaching.

Although the three kinds of functionaries are described as discrete types, in actual situations there may be considerable overlap among them. On the other hand, the scheme outlined above suggests that such attributes as public popularity and policy-making power need not reside in the same individual. For example, the dramatic leader who can attract members and con-

vince them of the importance of the movement and its
objectives may not be making the decisions with respect
to tactics, changes in organization, or even modification
of goals. True, his name comes to be closely identified
with the movement. Thus he—more than any other
single person—may become something of a symbol of
the movement and his conduct of considerable importance in attracting followers and cementing—or weakening—internal relationships. But other functionaries
can and do acquire power along with responsibilities
as the different positions inevitably become specialized
and diversified. While the role of the leader as a missionary or as a "front man" is directly related to the
movement's growth, other functionaries may aid or
spoil his efforts indirectly as they alter values and
goals for which he is supposed to stand. Not only are
power and privilege intrinsic in the operation of certain
offices in the formal structure of the movement; they
also flow from personal influence and esteem. Hence,
an informal structure of relationships develops.[3]

The leader—even if he is also the founder—may be
left in an impotent position so far as internal affairs
go, manipulated by strong bureaucratic functionaries.
One writer has pointed out in another connection that
these behind-the-scenes agents often possess professional skill and competence but little emotional stake
in an organization's avowed objectives. They may take
actions consistent chiefly with interests and problems
of their own roles, actions which have more and more
internal relevance and "which may result in the deflec-
tion of the organization from its original path which,
however, usually remains as the formally professed
aim of the organization." [4]

Just as they may act as a counterweight to the
leader, bureaucrats also hold a strategic position with

reference to the agitators. The latter, acting as human shuttles, carry the movement's message to the greater society and bring converts from the society into the movement. Though their work is directly relevant to the expansion of the movement and the attainment of its goals, their status provides them with little authority. For the most part, agitators do not compose the message they spread nor define the goals they try to popularize nor control the converts they secure; they are themselves supervised and directed by the bureaucratic tacticians and planners. One observer of diverse organizations has noted the tendency for conflict to develop between these two types of functionaries, each seeking to enhance his power on the basis of the activities peculiar to his role in the movement.[5] Needless to say, this working at cross-purposes can threaten the existence of a movement by weakening its internal machinery and by alienating members and potential members.

The preceding points can be summarized by the principle that some specialization of labor is essential if a movement is to grow. Internal chaos would result if each functionary were a jack-of-all-trades, and no movement under such circumstances could evolve beyond the incipient stage. While the dramatic leader may single-handedly bring many new members into the fold, extensive growth can occur only if his efforts are supplemented by a corps of agitators engaged in both promotion and proselyting. They, perhaps more than their bureaucratic colleagues, tend also to keep the movement flexible through their observation of and sensitivity to changing social conditions and public opinion.[6] While the agitator can often do no more than relay his impressions to the policy-makers, the needs and problems he uncovers would otherwise be submerged and neglected in the day-to-day routine of administration and pencil-pushing. Routine activities are not to be disparaged, however, nor are the bureaucrats in whose hands they rest. Removed from the public eye and devoid of glamour, making policy, keeping records, the bureaucrats provide the firm underpinnings of order and system around which the leader and agitator can drape such colorful appurtenances as idealism, emotion, and social protest.

Other sub-types of functionaries are recognizable among bureaucrats and agitators.[7] But the distinctions between leader, bureaucrat and agitator serve for present purposes, together with the recognition that the broad base of a movement's organization is made up of personnel, the rank-and-file members lacking special offices. The importance of the personnel resides not only in their number but in the fact that they, as much as the functionaries, come to be regarded as advocates of "the cause." Each member is a representative of the movement in the eyes of outsiders; whether he actively seeks converts or not his actions and general status in the society can in a measure aid or handicap the movement's growth.

Functionaries and personnel may lack or possess certain assets as advocates of a movement. Such an asset as social prestige, for example, can be extremely significant: "the prestige level at which a new element enters the society very largely determines the group of individuals to whom it may spread."[8] In the early days of Christian Science, for instance, when Mrs. Eddy was still an obscure preacher to tiny congregations, the converts were citizens of even greater obscurity and more limited accomplishments than their leader. After the movement had grown, and with it its founder's eminence, there followed the conversion of persons with increasingly high status in the fields of business, the theatre, and the professions (excepting medicine). On the other hand, although the ideals of Moral Rearmament have caught the interest of people whose eminence far exceeds that of Buchman, the movement's leader—among them John D. Rockefeller, Henry Ford, Harlan Stone, and Harry S. Truman[9]—interestingly, none of these prominent individuals has actually joined the movement. Of course, the effectiveness of an advocate is also dependent upon other attributes, such as his personality and the closeness or remoteness of his relations with potential acceptors.[10]

Group Cohesion Though a product of several other elements, especially tactics and structure, solidarity or cohesion within the movement is also a determinant of its growth. The leaders and agitators may succeed in winning supporters, but recruitment and agitation alone cannot forever sustain them without internal cohesion, *esprit de corps*. A movement torn by dissension, unable to present at least an appearance of internal tranquility to onlookers, will have hard going in trying to convert them—or to keep them, once converted.

There are various tactical and structural impediments to cohesion. For example, it may seem tactically wise at a given time to rally strength and support for an aggressive step toward some goal, or the mere consolidation of previous gains may appear more expedient. The problem of whether the aggressive or the conservative course should be taken has been estimated as the most common cause of internal conflict.[11] Margaret Sanger, for example, tells of returning from a European trip to find that the Birth Control League had settled down to relative inaction except for guarding its bank balance. The issues of using or saving its money, pushing the use of public clinics, and aggressively extending its membership beyond New York became so sharp that they eventually broke the movement in two.[12]

Internal cohesion is also greatly influenced by the distribution of power in a movement's structure and in the conduct of its functionaries. The individual official who is disloyal or attempts to subvert the organization to his own ends can often do it great damage. Especially are bureaucrats of the policy-making level in a singularly strategic position to benefit themselves and harm the movement. On the other hand, when he combines integrity with competence, the bureaucrat's main contribution to group unity often involves exercising his authority over the agitator. The latter's two most common official sins include deviating radically from established policy and thus upsetting long-range plans, on the one hand, and, on the other, acquiring undue popularity and a personal following which may enable him to wreck the movement by splintering its membership.

At least three techniques are commonly employed in fostering group morale and loyalty to the movement.[13] First, in-group loyalties are cultivated by an emphasis on ethnocentrism in the movement's ideology and tactics. Playing up a real or fancied enemy, contrasting the movement's values with contrary values in the society, linking the movement's goals and their superiority with the aspects of the *status quo* which are to be changed—these are devices that help to supplement the formal unity of membership with an emotional unity. A second means to internal cohesion is informal fellowship, friendly and intimate contacts in large or small groups and chiefly in leisure-time activities. Reliance upon small-group contacts is well illustrated in

Moral Rearmament's use of the house party, a pleasant gathering at a member's home where recreation and religion can be happily combined. Converts have said of these meetings, "We just get together and chat about Christ." These contacts are not only a manifestation of common membership but effectively generate and reinforce a consciousness of kind. A third technique for building *esprit de corps* is ceremony, which also provides personal contact, though usually on a formal level. Ceremonial behavior in small groups or in the mass (the parades, rallies, and mysterious rituals of the Ku Klux Klan, for instance) is another way of reminding the participant that he belongs and of reinforcing his feelings of identification with the movement.

Tactics Tactics probably comprise the element in social movements least in need of discussion as an influence on growth. Their relationship to the general survival of a movement is fairly clear and direct. They are also related to such elements as goals, ideology, and status system, for each of these can determine the kind of tactics which will or should be used. For instance, the bureaucrats are largely responsible for the choice of tactics, and once adopted, these tactics will call for a particular kind of agitator.

But apart from internal relatedness, the tactics employed in a given situation affect in a very direct way the reactions of outsiders to the movement as a whole. The tactics may pertain to goal-achievement or to proselyting. In both cases an evident relation exists between blunders and alienation on the one hand, between astuteness and sympathetic support on the other.

In general terms, the attributes of tactics which help

win supporters include: (1) utility with respect to goals; (2) realism concerning the cultural setting and changing social conditions, as well as a realistic differentiation between long-range and short-range objectives; and (3) developing needs where they are absent.

The first of these attributes, utility, simply involves a more particular application of the demonstrable utility of "means in general" as a stimulus to growth. Not that the achievement of *ultimate* goals is a critical factor; more important is concrete evidence that things are moving along, that tactics are—often by attaining more immediate goals—bringing closer the day when the "great changes" can be brought about. This evidence may appear in the fruits of successful legislative lobbying or favorable court decisions, in the elimination of competitors or the defeat of opponents, or in the altering of certain relationships and statuses in local communities. For example, while the Grange movement at its height did not substantially alter the standard of living of the farm population as a whole, in certain states it secured the passage of laws and developed cooperatives which many rural dwellers regarded as evidence that the movement was the answer to their economic ills.

The possibility of such "practical" attainment is enhanced by effective proselyting, for increased numbers mean that still more pressure can be applied in goal-achievement—especially if political channels are being utilized. Membership growth (operating in circular fashion) also becomes an asset to the very proselyting efforts which produce it; the old saying that "nothing succeeds like success" has a certain validity, though an outward impression of success can be as tactically significant in this respect as the genuine article.

Realism, the second desirable attribute of tactics,

sometimes involves utility but is not quite the same thing. Realism in one sense refers to the necessity for gearing tactics to the existing culture and hence appraising certain techniques on the basis of the public indignation or support they will arouse. Working within the existing system of basic laws, for example, is usually more realistic than ignoring those laws. The Ku Klux Klan's loss of popularity is certainly in part attributable to the floggings and murders which occurred in the name of Klan objectives, for violence and force are especially illegal in the modern state, which claims these as its own monopoly. (On the other hand, as the rise of Nazism demonstrated in Germany, violence and force are sometimes very productive tactics when adequate groundwork has been laid for their use.)

Realism must be maintained not only with respect to the cultural context in which a movement exists but also with respect to the fact that not all goals can be achieved by the same tactics. The latter point is particularly important as applied to ultimate and immediate goals. Long-range objectives require more preparation, often an extensive build-up, and premature efforts in their direction not only abort but can shatter a movement which has thus over-reached itself. The ill-fated cooperatives of the Grange are a case in point, for these were apparently developed as a shortcut to greater economic independence for the farmer. The effort was too broad in scope, however, and much too early in its timing. After this experiment in commerce the Grange declined rapidly, handicapped by this and other tactical blunders which grew out of the bureaucrats' failure or inability to control overly optimistic agitators and to provide policies designed for long-range expansion.

One writer pointing to the need for taking first steps first has suggested that the successful innovating group must begin by securing attention and must then justify its claims to leadership which, along with outmaneuvering competitors and combating opponents, may secure it "the confidence of the masses." [14] Simultaneously it must, of course, be developing those qualities which will enable it to use deftly the power it has sought for attaining ultimate objectives.

Implied in the above discussion is still another essential aspect of realism in tactics: that they be flexible. Despite the claims of many leaders of the gift of prophecy, social realities persistently elude the predictions of these "experts." Unforeseen obstacles, new opportunities, chances to exploit the mistakes of opponents —these and other circumstances are the product of so many uncontrollable agencies and forces that no set of tactics can be equally applicable to all times and all places. Efforts at bringing about changes in the civil rights of minorities and in legalizing the dissemination of birth-control information, as they have been turned with increasing effectiveness from legislative lobbying into judicial channels, illustrate this point.

A third attribute of tactics contributing to a movement's growth is the creation of needs where they are absent or the intensification of needs which already exist. It was earlier pointed out that one of the great assets for social movements is a social setting fraught with stress and crisis, factors conducive to favorable reception. The existence of such circumstances readymade by forces external to the movement is common enough but not inevitable in all areas of social life, nor is their intensity constant. A movement need not necessarily flounder, however, simply because social conditions are not bad enough to drive members into the fold. The point may be made again that in whatever way people interpret a situation, it is on the basis of that interpretation that they act. And one function of a movement's tactics is to lead people to define their life conditions so as to enhance the value of the movement in their eyes. Thus in the absence of a severe crisis, tactics may be used to make it *seem* that a crisis exists. In this way, the reasonably contented, apathetic outsider may be transformed into an anxious, dissatisfied individual more receptive to the movement than he would otherwise be. To turn this trick a wide variety of propagandistic and even rabble-rousing techniques are available. Whatever the devices employed by a movement's functionary, one of his guiding principles is to strive for the creation of a new desire for changes and a dissatisfaction with the status quo, either to create new feelings of deprivation in the minds of potential members or make old needs felt more strongly.[15]

The Ku Klux Klan after World War I provides an example of the technique of creating dissatisfaction. Though its campaign against Negroes, Catholics, and Jews was in part simply a matter of intensifying existing hatreds and prejudices, the vilification of minorities was also in part designed to instill in the unconverted the belief that these groups were responsible for his misfortunes, that his lot as a "true American" could be vastly improved by the suppression of these minorities, and that the Ku Klux Klan was the best means by which this could be done. Similarly, some who have joined Moral Rearmament did not realize they needed the services of its "soul surgeons" until brought by a friend to one of the informal meetings where confessions and testimonials are exchanged. Indeed, it is incumbent upon each member to bring a guest to the meetings, regardless of whether the latter feels any need for the movement's ministrations. The motto is "Woo, win, warn." [16]

The preceding discussion has not, of course, included all the attributes of social movements which are relevant to growth. It indicates, however, that a variety of ways exists in which each element can enhance or impede the acceptance of a movement—ignoring for the moment influences originating in the outside world. While all the component parts of a movement are directly related to its existence as a social system, certain ones (such as tactics and leadership) are more immediately related to actual growth than are others (such as ideology and internal cohesion). But no single element, not even leadership, is ever all-important in the career of a social movement. Research may ultimately enable the student of movements to appraise the various elements with precision and thus predict that their convergence in certain ways will result in the extinction, stagnation, or expansion of a movement.

6 External Influences on Growth

Shifting the emphasis from internal to external factors of growth means, in a sense, looking from the inside of social movements outward toward their social setting. Often these influences operate by amplifying or limiting the functions of the internal elements, whatever their intrinsic attributes may be.

Every movement occurs in a social setting, which, for present purposes, is seen as having two basic and interrelated dimensions: first, the structure of the society, especially the statuses, strata, subgroups and associations within it; second, the culture, consisting of the norms and values of the society.

In the study of social movements, the influence of external variables is seldom treated as explicitly or as fully as internal influences. Although an ill-directed movement with incompetent functionaries and unrealistic goals is probably doomed whatever the social setting, it is nevertheless unrealistic to view the internal elements as necessarily the most important determinants of its growth.

The flourishing social movement is the result of a congenial marriage between elements within the movement and external social conditions. In short, the conditions affecting its growth and the growth of any embryo, physical or social, are basically the same. If its own generative mechanism is seriously defective, the most favorable milieu can produce nothing; yet the most vigorous organism or organization remains dormant or dies in a milieu which provides it no nourishment.

The General Cultural Context

Cultural Consistency   One of the major dimensions of the social milieu—its cultural norms and values—bears a relationship to social movements which at first glance seems paradoxical. Some degree of consistency with the society's general culture is essential if a movement is to find acceptance. But how can there be compatibility with the very culture which the movement is committed to changing? This apparent contradiction is resolved by recalling that the mass society is characterized not by a neatly integrated culture but rather by a diversity of subcultures. And even though certain value-orientations (for example, success and equality) can be identified amid the heterogeneity of American society,[1] the fact remains that no movement need be compatible with *all* these society-wide orientations to be acceptable. Few movements have ever sought to change an entire society or, indeed, have had a relevance for every one of the major value configurations of that society.

Furthermore, these widely held values are usually expressed in such general terms that not only may they be achieved by many alternative methods but their inherent qualities are open to diverse interpretations. Although Americans generally agree on the importance of success, for example, the meaning of success and the definition of acceptable avenues to it are far from uniform in all quarters.

One other pertinent matter here is the distinction between ideals and actual behavior. This distinction is variously referred to as the normative versus the factual order, ideal versus real culture, or, in less technical language, precept versus practice. Rather than seek a change in ideals or norms, social movements often simply aim to bring social behavior into line with existing folkways and mores. Where this is the case the movement's general proposals, being quite congruent with the society's ideals, may well find very wide acceptance. But the spelling out of such proposals in the form of more specific goals (as when the Ku Klux Klan's program for Americanism is revealed as involving Protestant white supremacy) and the use of unacceptable means often creates apathy or hostility.

In considering the consistency of a movement with the existing culture, attention will here be focused chiefly on goals since it is especially in connection with goals that the problem arises. Much of what can be said regarding goals, however, is also applicable to ideology, tactics, and other means; their acceptability too is defined in part by cultural context.

The significance of compatibility between a movement and its surrounding culture varies with the phase of the culture which the movement proposes to alter. It is almost a sociological truism that in most industrial societies technological and scientific innovations are not only condoned but encouraged, and even in the realm of economic and political ideas there is considerable expectancy of change—though within limits. A movement whose proposals are incongruent with the status quo in these areas is less likely to generate opposition than one whose objectives involve such fields as sexual behavior, family life, and religion, where prevailing norms are often regarded as relatively immutable and absolute. (This "dogmatic" outlook, incidentally, may help account for the fact that though innovations in religion have not been lacking, they have usually nurtured only small cults; few have found wide enough acceptance for the building of a social movement. Movements concerned with political and economic ideas have probably been relatively much more numerous.) Inconsistencies, then, between existing societal norms and proposed objectives are more tolerable in certain areas of a culture than in others. But even where leeway exists, it is not limitless. Consistency and inconsistency do not comprise a dichotomy; they are matters of degree. Divorce, for example, is inconsistent with the Judaeo-Christian ideal of monogamy, but not so inconsistent as polygamy; hence the fate of classical Mormonism and the brisk prosperity of Reno, Nevada.

Thus the commonly held assumption that innovations inconsistent with existing culture stand little chance of being accepted is a misleading generalization. The latter view is but a partial truth, for cultural consistency is a conditional and not an absolute factor in selection. Additional research is needed regarding the more specific factors involved in consistency and the circumstances under which consistency becomes socially significant. Meanwhile, a concept of some analytical value is that of cultural drift.

Cultural Drift Drift is a concept borrowed from anthropology to describe the process "where minor alterations slowly change the character and form of a way of life, but where the continuity of the event is apparent."[2] The concept serves as a reminder that human beings live in a time dimension—as well as in a geographical and a social world—and that though social life is dynamic it is not without direction. Furthermore, the relationship between a movement and an existing culture can be so emphasized as to obscure another problem: that of the consistency of a movement with drifts or tendencies already under way (though perhaps not generally apparent) in some areas of that culture. Resistance to or acceptance of a new proposal may hinge largely on these pre-existing tendencies toward change rather than on long-established traditions.

The direction of cultural drift is sometimes not apparent because people characteristically preserve old symbols and stoutly defend norms even after actual behavior has moved on toward new patterns. Like the "great man" in history, an enterprising movement is rarely the original source of a social trend but rather capitalizes on an existing (though sometimes latent) one. Christian Science, for example, did not originate healing through faith, for this practice had a long history in Christianity. Furthermore, during the early decades of the movement's growth there was already a lively public interest in such phenomena as "animal magnetism," especially in New England where Christian Science was born. Movements often reformulate—as they incorporate—changes which are already in the air and awaiting an advocate. Again Christian Science provides an illustration. Some observers claim that the trend in American religion is an unreligious one, a trend toward secularism and pragmatism: Jesus as the Great Rotarian, bingo in the basement, and church membership as a cheap way of keeping up with the Joneses. If such a trend exists, Christian Science has, in some of its meanings, kept in step by interpreting material success as a spiritual achievement, emphasizing the infinite power of the individual, and thus reconciling economic ambitions and religious doctrines.[3] And although certain goals of a movement may seem to clash with traditional values, the conflict can be an asset because alteration of these very values may be inevitable and essential for the society's ultimate well-being or even its survival. Hence the difficulty of oppressing permanently "a movement whose aims are in harmony with tendencies of social change which are imminent in a given society." [4]

Form and Meaning While serious inconsistencies between a movement and its milieu may deter potential converts, it does not necessarily follow that apparent congruence makes for acceptance. Ultimate goals which are superficially acceptable and even laudatory by the standards of the culture may lend themselves to meanings which make them seem repugnant. Meanings, especially interpretations given to new proposals by potential acceptors, can condition and limit the significance of consistency quite as much as can cultural drift. For example, some citizens are sincerely dedicated to the general patriotic objectives of the Klu Klux Klan in the form in which they are sometimes expressed, but these same citizens have rejected the movement because the specific meanings the Klan often ascribes to these goals seem in themselves inhuman and unpatriotic.

The matter of cultural consistency as it pertains to acceptance and rejection cannot be discussed, therefore, merely in terms of the form of an innovation. The reception of an innovation will depend upon the meanings ascribed to it as well as upon its formal attributes, those attributes most immediately or readily apparent to the observer. The anthropologists especially have long stressed that when the form of a culture trait is adopted, it may be given quite a different meaning by the acceptor than it had for the donor—as when a wrist watch traded to a Pacific islander becomes a purely decorative object and its timekeeping ability is ignored. Acceptability may be enhanced by ascribing old meanings to new forms or by ascribing new meanings to old forms.[5] And the reason for such switching about is not hard to find, for a proposal must—to evoke a favorable reaction from potential acceptors—lend itself to identification and association with previous experience.[6] The critical question, then, is not whether the program of a movement coincides closely with the values of the culture but whether its proposals "make sense" to people on the basis of their cultural equipment.

In the case of social movements, however, lack or confusion of meaning is probably less often an obstacle to acceptance of a group's goals than it is for other kinds of innovations. There is this difference: most innovations are adopted through a process of unplanned diffusion, the borrowers interpreting and searching for meanings as best they can; but the goals of successful social movements are deliberately provided with interpretations (sometimes oddly diverse) by functionaries in the effort to make them magnetic as well as intelligible. The Ku Klux Klan is a case in point with its clarion call to red-blooded Southerners to defend the white South and its traditions from "mongrelization" and racial equality. At the same time the Klan has not hesitated, despite its fundamentally un-American goals, to appeal for the "re-establishment of great American principles" and the "development of the highest standard of citizenship," thus superficially tying itself in with widely held social verities. This process of interpreting goals thus goes even further when a carefully composed ideology or an astute functionary provides meanings which seem to resolve inconsistencies with existing cultural elements.

Proposed changes are often made to appear not only

meaningful and acceptable but essential; at the same time, the traditions these goals are designed to replace are interpreted by the movement as dispensable and obsolete. Moral Rearmament, for instance, made internationalism one of its major objectives just prior to World War II, a time when isolationism was especially strong in the United States. Self-centered, secular nationalism—despite its traditional tap-roots in American culture—was portrayed by the movement as the atavistic enemy of peace, and the movement's publication, *Rising Tide,* proclaimed that "Workers led by God can lead the World." Underscoring the indispensability of Moral Rearmament, Buchman in 1938 confronted two thousand followers at a meeting with the ultimatum, "America must rearm spiritually or all is lost!" And to an international convention at the Hague he summed up the situation thus: "Nationalism can unite a nation. Supernationalism can unite a world. God-controlled supernationalism is the only sure foundation for world peace." [7] Not all traditions will be shunned, of course. Some will be lauded and utilized (as Buchman repeatedly made belief in God central to his political slogans), and to these praiseworthy norms and values will be related certain meanings of the movement's objectives. A ring of familiarity and legitimacy is thus given to objectives whose meanings are linked either to society-wide or to local values.[8]

Differential Receptiveness of Subgroups

In Chapter One social heterogeneity and cultural confusion were described as conducive to an abundance of social movements in mass societies. A psychological concomitant, individual discontent, was also emphasized. It should again be noted that sociological and psychological facets of the mass society are demonstrably interrelated in the generating of social movements, that extraordinary disturbances to social and cultural equilibrium intensify the individual's frustrations and his search for their release. Among these disturbances are severe economic depression for a large segment of the population, mass migration or other major shifts in the population structure, and war and its aftermath. All are social changes tending to produce deep personal bewilderment and dissatisfactions, and some of their effects were explored in the discussion of crisis in Chapter Four.

The very heterogeneity, however, which contributes to the general proliferation of movements also accounts for the fact that not all the members of a society are equally receptive to their appeal. While most citizens of a modern society will agree that it can be improved by changes, they will invariably disagree over what changes are needed or needed most. And rarely will those who subscribe to the same changes be unanimous on how these may best be brought about. Though the reasons for such disagreement are varied and often elusive, the mere existence of dissension rules out the possibility of any social movement appealing to all adults in a society, especially in a mass society where the disagreement is uniquely intensified by extreme specialization of knowledge, activities and statuses.* Therefore, social structure, particularly as it involves a variety of economic, ethnic, religious, and racial subgroups, must be considered one of the important dimensions of the social setting having an influence on

* An interesting diagram by R. M. MacIver and Charles H. Page[9] suggests the multiplicity of group affiliations characterizing the individual in the mass society and the manner in which intimacy of relations declines as group size increases.

the career of a movement. Of the many ways the structural element is related to selection, only a few can be touched on here.

In considering reactions to social movements, a portion of the society can be ignored simply because there are always people who are unaware (or vaguely aware) that a given movement exists. Among the rest of the people reactions will vary from favorable to unfavorable, from acceptance to rejection. Midway are the apathetic individuals. Admitting the crudeness of this acceptance-rejection scheme, it is nevertheless a helpful device for pointing up the relevance of certain differences between subgroups to a movement's growth.

Some Reasons for Diverse Receptiveness   Anthropologist Ralph Linton, in dealing with the general problem of diffusion, observed that new proposals or practices are "rarely of a sort which can be useful to all the members of all existing categories or compatible with all the constellations of functionally interrelated culture elements associated with various categories. This means that the dissemination of most elements is selective." [10] The same writer also has suggested that in the matter of acceptance "the prestige level at which the new element enters the society very largely delimits the group of individuals to whom it may spread." [11]

The differential appeal of movements for various subgroups in a society serves to underscore what was said earlier about the process of selection in social change: even the most popular innovations do not win approval from all quarters of the society simultaneously. Typically, they find acceptance in one segment at a time, spreading from one subgroup to another in a process of intersocietal transmission similar in many ways to the diffusion of culture traits between societies. Therefore, the problem of why a movement may find popularity with some subgroups and encounter indifference or resistance from others can be illuminated by considering certain influences associated with intersocietal diffusion.

In this connection, of course, the functional value to a social movement of one of its traits may vary in time and place. For instance, extremely aggressive tactics may make a movement appealing to one subgroup but render it repugnant to another, thus both enhancing and reducing its chances for survival. So far no method is available for appraising the net balance of elements which are thus simultaneously functional and dysfunctional. (As Merton has pointed out, evolving canons for such assessments in the functional analysis of any area or problem is one of the important challenges to sociology.[12])

Returning to Linton's propositions, the influence of the factors he describes—utility, compatibility, and prestige—is as relevant to social movements as to other innovations. But Linton was dealing with relatively homogeneous folk societies, and his generalizations require modification when applied to the more complex mass societies. His three conditions for acceptance must be viewed in the context of a variety of subgroups, each with problems, norms, and values that are often distinctive and sometimes unique. To be specific, various regions in the United States possess some problems, and even certain norms, which are somewhat peculiar to themselves. So do various occupational groupings and social classes. The cleavage between religious groups is largely a matter of normative differences, occasionally a matter of prestige. Frustrations faced by some ethnic and racial segments are not shared by others.

As an illustration of the significance of norms, the program of a relatively new movement (Congress on Racial Equality) to press for racial equality through persistent but non-violent techniques is repugnant to many white Americans, especially in the South, but it is quite compatible with the values and aspirations of most Negroes, Indians, and other racial minorities. Linton's second variable, prestige level, is probably most often manifest in the influence of class status; for example, the blue-collar members of some labor movements have been viewed with condescension by most white-collar workers, although the latter might long ago have profited in practical ways through union membership. Similarly, a movement's utility, Linton's third factor, is measured by the standards of particular subgroups—as is shown in the rejection of the farmers' Grange movement by urban dwellers who, far from gaining by its program, might have suffered a rise in their cost of living had it been a complete success. At a given time and for a given area of life, some subgroups more than others clearly have a stake in the status quo.

Social Rank   Social rank comes into operation if and when a social movement is identified with some particular prestige level or social class. For instance, during the depression of the 1930's, Technocracy was thought of as a movement for intellectuals; the Molly McGuires of the 19th century were viewed as lower-class ruffians by many Americans; and such movements as Feminism and Christian Science have been regarded as characteristically middle class. Not that outsiders always make conscious judgments on this score. On the contrary, there may be only the vaguest feeling of looking up to or down upon (or across at) the functionaries and members of a movement. In some instances a movement cannot be ranked at all clearly in this fashion because it cuts through several social strata (as did the Grange, for example) but when ranking is possible, it helps determine which subgroups will respond favorably and which unfavorably.

Interestingly, even in preliterate societies innovations may be resisted or adopted to the extent that they are associated with groups of a particular rank: some members of the Badaga tribe in India have supported proposals to change certain rituals involving music because musicians are ranked very low in a caste system which they wish to emulate.[13] The occasional influence of stratification on the acceptance of social movements is well illustrated in the case of Father Divine's Peace Mission movement whose early members were predominantly, perhaps exclusively, lower-class Negroes. The bulk of the membership continues to be Negro, though there are a few whites, some of whom have disregarded the barriers of class and caste alike in order to join. It is notable too, that the whites appear to be Northerners. Such cases illustrate the generalization that a proposal will be adopted somewhat more readily if it is identified with people who are admired rather than with those who discounted or despised.[14]

The operation of social rank with respect to the acceptance and rejection of movements should not, of course, be oversimplified. For one thing, diffusion of innovations in mass societies has also moved from groups of lower status to those of higher status. During the last 150 years, for example, styles of costume common to the European upper classes have been abandoned by them for styles more in line with lower-class dress, and the cosmetics and short hair once a monopoly of sexually casual women have been adopted by those more conventional and respected.[15] The popularity among all classes in the United States of jazz, swing, and dance forms of lower-class origin also come to mind in this connection.

Further complicating the operation of social rank is the fact that judgments made concerning the relative social status of others may be based, on the one hand, upon "corporate class consciousness" or, on the other hand, upon "competitive class feeling." [16] The former is simply a consciousness of kind, a feeling of belonging with people in a given class and of upholding its interests and standards—as sometimes occurs, for example, among "the workers" or among "the old families." Competitive class feeling, by contrast, is a personalized and specific feeling of superiority (or inferiority) to another individual with whom one may be competing for recognition and advancement; hence, the need for conspicuous display and consumption of goods. Since corporate class consciousness is common only at the extreme ends of the class range in this country, the social status of members of a movement must be distinctly either high or low to be significant in the recruitment of new members. As previously pointed out, the original followers of Father Divine were markedly lower class, and though middle-class Negroes (and whites) have joined him, they remain proportionately very few.

Still another reason why the influence of social rank is not greater than it is lies in the tendency of most Americans to profess middle-class status and to display middle-class sentiments. Especially relevant here are the sentiments involving a denial that class differences exist or are significant and the emphasis on competition and emulation,[17] attributes designed to reduce the significance of social position as an influence in conversion to a social movement.

A last circumstance modifying the influence of social rank is that the mutual ranking of subgroups does not necessarily result in neat, "higher-lower" dichotomies. Rarely is any group (or individual, for that matter) ascribed with prestige regarding all its attributes.[18] Students of stratification have frequently pointed out, for example, that although middle-class residents may regard with awe and envy the leisure-time associations and superior social standing of the upper class, the sexual behavior of the latter may simultaneously be viewed critically and with distaste.

A quality of American class structure, however, which very possibly has not operated adversely for social movements is the frequent lack of correspondence between ideals and actual behavior, or, in the words of MacIver and Page:

> the "inconsistency" between the economic-class structure, within which vertical mobility is limited, the competitive-psychological values of many, perhaps most, individuals in American society constitutes a situation that has an important bearing on such phenomena as the rise of and susceptibility to those social movements the programs of which "explain" the discrepancy and promise its removal and the possibly increasing degree of psychological disturbances among middle-class-minded but economically frustrated sections of the population.[19]

Compatibility of Norms The discussion earlier in the chapter of general cultural consistency is largely applicable here with respect to the second variable, namely, the compatibility between a movement's goals and the normative structure of particular subgroups. To be sure, there are certain large, social-ethical principles which are roughly subscribed to by most members of a mass society. These principles are variously described as common ultimate ends, value-orientations, or as the expressions of a society's ethos. As previously suggested, however, they by no means compose a perfectly integrated value-structure or a code of completely consistent norms. On the contrary, "complex division of labor, regional variations, ethnic heterogeneity, and the proliferation of specialized institutions and organizations all tend to insulate differing values from one another." [20]

Since subgroups vary in their standards of what is proper and important, social movements may embrace proposals which would be incongruent with the standards of one subgroup but perfectly congenial with those of another. Movements therefore face two criteria of cultural acceptability: the broad normative code of the society as a whole and the various codes of subgroups within the society. The chance of acceptance is, of course, greatly increased when some of the objectives and activities of a movement are consistent with norms of the general society and are also compatible with norms peculiar to certain subgroups. For example, though some aspects of Father Divine's movement are incongruous with American ideals, such others as racial equality and human brotherhood are consistent with the broad stream of our traditions and political proclamations. Likewise, Moral Rearmament, in its past and current appeals for Christlike living, has developed general goals and beliefs in no way contrary to those of most Western societies, but in certain tactics, rituals, and detailed rules of living it has manifested a greater consistency with Protestantism than with other faiths.

Finally, it may be said that the values and norms of

the subgroups to which an individual belongs are often seen by him as more closely related to his personal welfare and satisfactions than the norms and values of the society as a whole, which by contrast seem remote and elusive.[21] Therefore, it may be generalized that a lack of consistency between a movement's proposals and the norms of subgroups toward whom these proposals are especially directed is a much more serious obstacle to growth than is an incompatibility involving norms common to the total society.

Apparent Utility* The effects of social rank and cultural compatibility are sometimes altered by still another factor, apparent utility, itself a major, direct influence on the receptiveness of subgroups to innovations. Reactions to a new law or local ordinance, for instance, seem to be governed as often by "practical considerations" of various groups as by their codes of ethics. Utility has several implications for the selection of proposals sponsored by social movements. Since the attainment of movements' goals involves changing certain phases of the existing social order, among the various subgroups confronted with this possibility some will be inclined to react favorably, others unfavorably. The

---

* Apparent utility is intentionally distinguished here from function. The function of an element is its contribution to the survival and welfare of a group, organization or individual,[22] and implicit in the concept is the idea that an objective and presumably valid judgment has been or can be made concerning that contribution. By apparent utility, on the other hand, is meant the *assumed* usefulness of an element; thus the concept involves a subjective and sometimes erroneous judgment or belief held by the individual or group considering the element. It follows, of course, that a movement which has apparent utility for a given subgroup may or may not prove actually functional for it. Nevertheless, belief in the movement rather than the movement's objectively assessed performance is crucial in gaining and holding members.

subgroups which believe they will lose by such a change, which have the largest vested interest in the status quo, will be likely to oppose the movement if they can. To them the movement's proposals seem not only without utility but positively detrimental. Other subgroups may be quite indifferent to the movement because of their belief that its efforts will be neither disadvantageous nor beneficial. Or if they react at all, it is because of factors other than utility. Still other subgroups may feel that they not only have nothing to lose by the proposed change but may actually benefit by it.

The groups for whom the movement appears to have utility are, of course, a likely source of converts and supporters unless disadvantages arise in connection with cultural compatibility or social rank. Labor movements, for instance, in going through the process of selection, have usually exhibited the same well known pattern over and over. They find widest acceptance by the subgroups most likely to gain from unionization, the various categories of blue-collar workers; they have been most actively opposed by employers whose status brings the privileges and rights most likely to be impaired by the movements; mild opposition or complete apathy has been the usual reaction of farmers, white-collar workers, and other economic groups whose involvement in the issues has been more remote and who have variously seen themselves as being only slightly injured or quite unaffected by unionization. Whether labor unions are inherently "good" or "bad," whether their effect on the total society is detrimental or beneficial, are questions unlikely either to receive sincere consideration or to be the real basis for various subgroups' support, opposition, or indifference with respect to unionization.

As in judging relative social status, the judgments made by individuals or whole groups regarding a movement's utility may be, and often are, erroneous. But, once more, behavior is largely determined by the judgment itself and not its validity. In summary, an individual's assessment of a movement's objectives when he regards them from a pragmatic—rather than a normative—point of view is largely a consequence of one or more of his statuses: his enthusiasm, opposition, or apathy will in part reflect his membership in subgroups based on occupation, sex, income, region, race, and so forth.

A special word should be added regarding indifference, for the silent walls of public apathy are probably as great an impediment to the growth of social movements as are active, vocal opposition. Individuals who are self-employed, for instance, can see little benefit and also little personal disadvantage for themselves in union-sponsored legislation pertaining to bargaining methods. Similarly, an indifferent outlook toward new sects may be found among the devoted members of tolerant religious groups: no effort is made to oppose and none to assist the embryo movements. Not all the reasons for apathy are obvious, but lack of involvement because of one's statuses and roles is a common and fairly evident one.

Unconcern is usually widespread when a movement is still at the innovation stage because so many people are unaware that it exists—or, having become aware of it, fail to see in the movement any meaning or significance for themselves. But mass apathy gradually gives way to a wide range of reaction: as the movement employs more aggressive tactics and the implications of proposals become more apparent, some of the subgroups previously indifferent to the movement inevitably swing away from neutrality toward a stand that is either receptive or antagonistic.[23] During its earlier years, for example, the Grange showed little growth, not because of active opposition but because of disinterest. When more dramatic and materialistic goals were adopted along with vigorous tactics, the number of converts quickly swelled. So did the number of opponents, as railroad, financial, and manufacturing executives began to grumble about the Grange's danger to capitalism. And these interest groups soon translated their apprehensions into political and economic action.

Understandably, hostility flowers early among subgroups which believe most strongly that their vested interests are endangered by the movement. The campaign of an organized opposition may succeed in winning to its banner some apathetic subgroups by making it appear that these too have vested interests at stake. Those who come late to such a decision after a relatively long period of disinterest are likely, according to one student of social change, however, to contribute little fervor or stability to the opposition since their resistance is largely nominal and ritualistic.[24]

It should be made clear at this point that vested interests extend beyond economic matters. A subgroup may feel that it has vested interests in a political system, in civil rights, in a certain source of prestige, or indeed, in any system of privileges and rights bound up with the competition for status, power, and reputation.[25] The frequent observation that a group opposes certain proposals because it fears the changes as threats to its security fails to point out that *particular* elements in the existing order especially seem to assure security to a given group. For example, considerable opposition to medical advances has come from physicians with established reputations which might well be placed in jeopardy if traditional techniques should prove wrong and the new ones prove right.[26] When technical authority is questioned or shown to have been mistaken, the prestige which goes with possessing such authority amounts to a vested interest under assault. Clearly, when a movement is so organized and oriented that its appeal for a subgroup is enhanced by all three of the above elements (rank, norms, and utility), their operation is functional in that the likelihood of support from that subgroup is at a maximum; the greater the number of subgroups of which this would be true, the more extensive will be the movement's growth. On the other hand, the three variables may, instead of reinforcing each other, operate in contrary fashion, the functions for the movement of one being offset by the dysfunctions or detrimental effects of another. The relative importance of each to the others cannot be predicted when a movement is unacceptable to a subgroup on one count (such as cultural compatibility) but on another (such as apparent utility) is highly appealing. A case in point is the movement of the United World Federalists for an international government strong enough to suppress war. The merit of such an objective is evident to nearly all Americans, but to many citizens the surrender of some national sovereignty seems to be an unpatriotic denial of our independence and integrity.

In conclusion, it should be noted that the effects on a movement of apparent utility and social rank can be either functional or dysfunctional: each factor is capable of evoking active interest in and support of a movement or, on the other hand, of alienating a subgroup so as to preclude interest or support. The influence exerted by compatibility of norms, however, is usually either inconsequential or is dysfunctional. That is, though incompatibility impedes the popularity of a movement, compatibility merely facilitates the operation of other factors; in itself it can hardly be said to generate enthusiasm or interest.

7 Purposes and Consequences

In the pioneering days of American sociology, William Graham Sumner berated experts and laymen alike for failing to distinguish clearly between human purposes and consequences. The consequences of men's actions, he thundered, bear no necessary resemblance —indeed may be quite contrary—to the ends toward which they strive.[1] Other social scientists have made the same point and, as in the case of Sumner, still go unheeded for the most part. The distinction between purposes and consequences is especially vital in the study of social movements. Here men formulate objectives, sometimes grandiose ones; they organize and plan in order to attain these goals. But their "best laid plans" can go astray. Perhaps the most innocuous outcome of a movement that misfires is merely failure to reach its professed goals. More disturbing both to the planners and to the society is a tendency to produce consequences which were never foreseen. Such results may be only indirectly related or quite unrelated to the original goals, but, being unanticipated, they are invariably upsetting. More awkward still, the consequences may be actually contrary to the movement's aims: the Eighteenth Amendment is a classic example of this wry possibility.

Accidental Influences

If the historian can be accused of often giving the accidental element too much prominence in human events, perhaps the sociologist can be accused of giving it too little. Anthropologists are sometimes more sensitive to fortuitous factors and frequently report this kind of occurrence: the British in India decided to lay out a parade ground where certain members of the famously polyandrous Toda tribe maintained the sacred dairies of their buffalo cult. Moving the dairy stripped it of its sacred significance and undermined the cult's ritual. "The amputation of dairy ritual, unintentional though it was, affected the economic life of this group, weakened the cohesiveness of the whole culture, and made possible the infiltration of new elements." [2] Obviously, no one could have forecast this particular action by the British authorities—although an observer acquainted with Toda culture could have anticipated some of the ramifications of the action once it was decided upon. So too with social movements. Fortuitous events occur within a movement or outside it which the scientist cannot predict simply because he can never be in command of every detail. Yet such events can give a movement tremendous impetus or mortally damage its chances for growth.

To refer to such events as "accidents" is not to imply that they lack determinants or causes or even that the determinants are beyond discovery. Rather, these events are simply phenomena which cannot ordinarily be anticipated with the knowledge which is actually and presently at hand.[3] An accident in this sense is often the product of a convergence of factors which occurs so rapidly that there is no time for the kind of analysis necessary for prediction; often it results from decisions —perhaps impulsively made—by individuals or small groups whose power or position is such that they can significantly alter the life of other people but whose motives and intentions elude examination. In the study of social change the discovery of determinants is often made in retrospect, and therefore they often appear infinitely more obvious than they were prior to an event. Such discovery also leads to the serious fallacy of assuming that certain individuals were responsible for the event and that they acted with a foresight and understanding which in fact they did not possess. Claiming or ascribing unearned credit of this kind has been aptly referred to as "rationality after the act." [4] This fallacy links consequences inextricably with purposes; it assumes falsely that the observed results were intended to come about as they did.

An example of the fortuitous element is found in the impetus given Christian Science just after the turn of the century by the publicity following a suit which was filed against Mrs. Eddy's associates. Certain so-called heirs, apparently prodded by a newspaper scenting a good story, claimed she was mentally incompetent and being exploited by selfish assistants. The widely publicized court ruling vindicated the assistants, and, by implication, Mrs. Eddy's mental faculties. In its wake came a wave of public applause suggesting that not only had the trial advertised the existence of the movement to a large new segment of the population but also that the prestige and popularity of Christian Science and its aged founder had been considerably enhanced.

In the case of the Grange, an unforeseen adverse element appeared in the form of competing movements:

the Farmers' Alliance especially seemed to help in crippling the Grange's state and local chapters as farmers in all regions shifted their allegiance because—according to many of them—they could thus enjoy equal benefits for cheaper dues. That such a competitor would be a serious threat is predictable enough, but the accidental element lies in the actual emergence of the competitor.

The Ku Klux Klan too has been subject to accidental influences, favorable and otherwise. One student of the movement has suggested, for instance, that "The Birth of a Nation" (an all-time classic of the silent screen) may have contributed much to the Klan's popularity since the film, seen by 50% of all urban adults in the United States, vividly condemned Reconstruction, exaggerated Negro ascendence, and portrayed the Klan in a favorable light.[5] On the other hand, the movement suffered serious damage to its prestige because of the unanticipated trial in 1925 of its Indiana Grand Dragon who was convicted of raping and causing the death of his secretary. Immediately after this sensational event both the Republican and Democratic parties, previously silent about the movement, disclaimed any relationship with the hooded empire.

Another and more recent example is socialism in the United States. Many of its reforms were ultimately embodied in the New Deal, and, instead of becoming a rallying ground for the unemployed and underprivileged during the 1930's, the movement continued declining to its present state of near oblivion. Moral Rearmament almost suffered a similar fate when the eruption of World War II rendered its support of internationalism and pacifism somewhat anachronistic; as an additional blow, members of the movement in England and the

United States were refused exemption from military service. One of the most dramatic cases, however, of unexpected events affecting a movement—in this instance through its leader—was the trial of Father Divine in 1932 for disturbing the peace of Sayville, Long Island. His arrest by itself brought the Peace Mission movement more publicity than could otherwise have been had. Father Divine's charge of racial persecution also brought liberals all over the nation to his support. Moreover, a member of the movement had sounded the ominous warning that the unfriendly judge "don' know who he monkeyin' with," [6] and the single event in the whole affair which guaranteed Divine the loyalty of old followers and also many new converts was the judge's death four days after he had sentenced Father to a year in jail.

The existence of fortuitous influences of this kind does not mean, of course, that they should be inflated beyond their importance. In the first place, their operation is by no means as constant as it sometimes seems with regard to a particular program or venture such as a social movement. In the second place, even when they do occur, accidental influences are not usually crucial and often play a role distinctly subordinate to forces which are somewhat better understood and more predictable. Third, with the growth of knowledge and techniques, various types of events and relationships in the field of social change which were once regarded as mysterious and capricious have been—and will continue to be—brought increasingly within scientific understanding and prediction. Even so, sufficiently numerous events will continue to elude prediction and accurate explanation to justify the use of *accidental influences* in the analysis of social movements.

Manifest and Latent Consequences

The failure of human undertakings to work out as intended may be approached in still another light, one which does not emphasize the accidental element. Certainly there are occurrences which are unforeseen by most people though they are not unforeseeable for the scientist, occurrences that are not especially sudden and do not stem from acts of personal whim but from traditional patterns of relationships, norms, and behavior. Sometimes an agency of change such as a social movement employs established means for the purpose of producing certain consequences, but quite different ones occur. The results thus brought about may be not only unanticipated but unwanted, and their occurrence may even go unrecognized. But in any event, the distinguishing feature of these effects is that they depart, sometimes most dramatically, from the results intended by their initiators. In the case of social movements, their various internal elements may, by producing unintended effects, not only impede the attainment of explicit goals but endanger the very existence of the movements themselves.

While more technical terms are sometimes employed in this connection, it is sufficient here to distinguish *manifest consequences* (those which are foreseen and are explicitly intended) from *latent consequences* (those which are not explicitly intended and are presumably unforeseen).* If it is assumed that very few social

* Probably the best analysis of this subject is by Robert Merton[7], whose terminology has been modified in the present discussion. It is interesting that in the case of social movements, latent consequences are fairly easily distinguished from manifest consequences since there is always some explicit statement of purposes available as a yardstick; observable re-

movements deliberately seek self-injury, it may be said that manifest consequences are usually beneficial to the movement while latent consequences may be either beneficial or harmful.

Some of the latent consequences which accompany a movement's development occur within the movement itself and seem chiefly to affect goals, internal organization, or membership growth. For example, social movements—along with other kinds of organizations—tend to develop an informal structure in the course of meeting day-to-day problems and situations, a structure which differs from the formally established system of offices and specialized jobs. Although this informal structure often aids in the attainment of objectives, it is sometimes responsible for the abandoning or modifying of original goals.[8] The Grange is an especially illuminating case here, since very early in its career effective control moved from the hands of original top officeholders out to the grass-roots functionaries, while at the same time the shift in goals occurred which transferred emphasis from fraternal and educational to economic and political objectives. (Interestingly, the shift has now gone full circle, with the modern Grange again dedicated largely to fraternal and educational aims.) The Ku Klux Klan of Reconstruction days, of course, also originated as a fraternal organization and was transformed even more quickly than the Grange into something very different. Christian Science, in contrast to the Klan and the Grange, has proceeded much more in accordance with the plans of its founder. Although Mrs. Eddy failed to anticipate the emergence

---

sults of a movement's activities which deviate from that yardstick are latent consequences. In the case of other kinds of associations or agencies the distinction is not so readily made since purposes may be obscure, varied, or lacking consensus.

of several apostate leaders in branch churches, she assiduously tightened up the organization when splinter sects did appear and none ever became a serious competitor. Indeed, to a remarkable degree the movement's goals, ideology, status system, and tactics have gone unaltered since the death of Mrs. Eddy half a century ago.

One ironic possibility confronting movements has been mentioned before: an apparently unanticipated and rarely desired outcome of achieving goals can be the abrupt demolition of the whole organization. Unless additional objectives are devised, the movement lies robbed of its reason for existence.

When a movement is successful in attaining one or more of its goals, these manifest consequences obviously involve some altering of the general society. Changes may also occur in the society, however, as latent consequences of a movement's activities. Such unexpected accomplishments are, of course, similar to the almost endless, unanticipated results of material inventions such as the auto and radio. The unplanned (and sometimes unwanted) effects of these last have been widely recognized inside and outside social science, but the similarly unforeseen ramifications of social movements have received little attention. Doubtless a vast number of unexpected results attend every movement but most are never recorded. Often these come about after the movement's own activities have diminished or ended. And the latent consequences a movement stores up for some subgroups in the society will be very unlike the effects eventually felt by others.

For instance, among the Grange's unanticipated byproducts may be counted its tremendous ideological influence on later farm organizations[9] and its improvement of relations between farmers and businessmen.

Business executives discovered that the rural dwellers were not helpless or passive, and the farmers learned, through their own failures in cooperatives, a new tolerance for industrialists.[10] Another case in point has been the movement for birth control which, in the United States, was originally founded to relieve poverty-stricken and undernourished mothers in the slum areas from an endless succession of births they could ill afford either financially or physically. For most of its forty-year history in this country, however, the movement's message (planned parenthood) and its materials (literature and contraceptives) have been accepted more widely and enthusiastically by the middle classes than by the lower classes for whom they were primarily designed. Unplanned or at least unformulated results stem not only from goal-achievements but from the means employed in seeking such goals. An example is the Klan's use of and influence on the ballot resulting in its political dominance in at least five states in 1924 which in turn facilitated political manipulations quite unrelated to Klan ideology and goals. Similarly, the Grange's ventures in business enterprises were simply tactical means which, when they aborted, proved disastrous to the movement itself.

The subject of latent consequences has still different implications when viewed with respect to individual members rather than the movement as a whole. What a person "gets" out of his participation may have little or nothing to do with avowed objectives and creeds. As pointed out in Chapter Four, for example, functionaries may—and often do—reap all sorts of material and psychological benefits never revealed to the rank and file. The "rake-off" in its crudest forms has contaminated movements with the loftiest of ideals. So too have internal autocracy and tyranny. Less often are illegitimate material gains enjoyed by ordinary members though occasionally (as in the case of the Ku Klux Klan) they too have opportunities to soil their hands for personal advantage. When incidental benefits become more rewarding for ordinary members than the movement's explicitly promised satisfactions, its functionaries may find themselves in a quandary, the same quandary which has often faced religious missionaries offering material gifts to the heathen as an inducement to accept spiritual ones. In short, the material and non-material come to be closely identified, as suggested in the classic manifesto of one backsliding American Indian tribe: "No more blanket, no more hallelujah!"

But advantages unrelated to goals need not be of a material kind. Probably emotional satisfactions account in large part for conversion and continued loyalty in most movements, and often they occur as latent rather than manifest consequences. Because of these intangible compensations, it is of little use for the social scientists or others to point out to members that there may be more effective ways than through the movement of achieving certain ends or even to suggest that a given movement stands no chance of attaining its avowed objectives at all. For as one psychologist has observed, "men and women rarely are able to wish to be social scientists." [11] Rather than any fervent dedication to a movement's proposals, merely the satisfaction of belonging to something can become the basic bond, or perhaps the emotional stimulus of the ritual or the simple pleasurable fellowship of small and intimate groupings. In so far as movements provide a feeling of in-group membership and of intimacy through association formerly enjoyed in the small community and local neighborhood, "they create little oases of intimate social cohesion in the midst of that vast expanse T. S.

Eliot has called the Wasteland." [12] The ceremonial degree-granting and leisure-time activities of the Grange, the Wednesday night testimonial meetings of Christian Science, the awesome rituals and silent secrecy of the Klan—all must be credited with helping to draw and retain members. Yet the elation, recognition, and pleasure derived from these activities are nowhere promised in the statements of purpose. They are latent consequences. And acceptance of a movement often occurs in part because the movement is seen as a requirement for getting something which is desired but not expressedly embodied in its objectives. [13]

Social Movements and Social Change

Several assertions were made at the beginning of this study about the significance of social movements. They may well be repeated here in the light of the case material and analysis presented in this book. The point was made that movements constitute an important sociological subject because they have become numerous in mass societies and collectively embrace vast numbers of people. Beyond their numerical significance, however, lie more fundamental implications. A movement, being in some ways a society in miniature, comprises a social system manageable in size for the study of certain aspects of social structure—for instance, bureaucracy, leadership, large and small group relations, and so forth.

Furthermore, social movements provide virtually a bottomless pit of empirical materials well-suited for explorations in the field of social change. While the application of concepts already available in this field will further an understanding of movements (and perhaps even facilitate predictions concerning their individual destinies), their continued study will simultaneously extend the theoretical and conceptual equipment which needs to be brought to bear on still other change-related topics. The double relevance of movements for this purpose is rooted in the fact that, first of all, each movement constitutes an innovation; knowing more about the careers of movements, we shall know more also about the processes of selection and integration of innovations in general. Second, since thriving movements—and sometimes those less robust—exert a detectable influence upon the society in which they occur, their analysis can provide the social scientists with greatly needed principles about the rate, direction, and consequences of social changes. Simultaneously, the study of movements can also illuminate for the social planner the possibilities and problems of instituting social change by blueprint.

FOOTNOTES

CHAPTER 1

[1] Bernard Barber, "Acculturation and Messianic Movements," *American Sociological Review,* Vol. 6 (1941), pp. 663-669.

[2] Robert K. Merton, *Social Theory and Social Structure,* Glencoe, Ill.: Free Press, 1949, p. 50.

[3] Hadley Cantril, *The Psychology of Social Movements,* New York: John Wiley and Sons, 1941, p. 10.

[4] John W. Bennett and Melvin M. Tumin, *Social Life,* New York: Alfred A. Knopf, 1949, p. 612.

[5] Herbert Blumer, "Elementary Collective Behavior," *New Outline of the Principles of Sociology* (Alfred McClung Lee, *ed.*), New York: Barnes and Noble, 1951, pp. 172-173.

[6] Margaret Mead, *Coming of Age in Samoa,* New York: William Morrow and Company, 1928, pp. 202-203. Reprinted with the publisher's (Copyright, 1928) permission.

[7] Cantril, *op. cit.,* p. 49.

[8] Merton, *op. cit.,* p. 127.

[9] Cantril, *op. cit.,* p. 59.

[10] Leo Lowenthal and Norbert Guterman, *Prophets of Deceit,* New York: Harper and Brothers, 1949, p. 17.

[1] Cantril, *op. cit.,* p. 64.

CHAPTER 2

[1] Carl C. Taylor, *The Farmers' Movement: 1620-1920,* New York: American Book Company, 1953, p. 499.

[2] These definitions appear, respectively, in Rudolf Heberle, "Observations on the Sociology of Social Movements," *American Sociological Review,* Vol. 14 (1949), p. 349; and Herbert Blumer, "Elementary Collective Behavior," *New Outline of the Principles of Sociology* (Alfred McClung Lee, *ed.*), New York: Barnes and Noble, 1951, p. 199.

[3] Blumer, *ibid.,* pp. 212-213.

[4] This distinction between coordinated and uncoordinated movements is similar in some ways to Blumer's distinction between specific and general movements. *Ibid.,* pp. 200-203.

[5] Rudolf Heberle, *Social Movements,* New York: Appleton-Century-Crofts, 1951, p. 25.

[6] Thomas H. Greer, *American Social Reform Movements,* New York: Prentice-Hall, 1949, p. 276.

[7] Blumer, *op. cit.,* pp. 212-213.

[8] Edward A. Kimball, *Lectures and Articles on Christian Science,* Chesterton, Ind.: E. K. Wait, 1921, pp. 379-384, 402, 453.

[9] Theodore Abel, "The Pattern of a Successful Political Movement," *American Sociological Review,* Vol. 2 (1937), p. 349.

[10] Ernest S. Bates and John V. Dittemore, *Mary Baker Eddy,* New York: Alfred A. Knopf, 1932, p. 313.

[11] Max Weber, *The Theory of Social and Economic Organization* (translated by A. M. Henderson and Talcott Parsons), New York: Oxford University Press, 1947, pp. 358-360.

[12] Rilma Buckman, "Social Engineering: A Study of the Birth Control Movement," *Social Forces,* Vol. 22 (1944), p. 422.

CHAPTER 3

[1] Carl A. Dawson and Warner E. Gettys, *An Introduction to Sociology* (3rd ed.), New York: Ronald Press, 1948, p. 690.

[2] Margaret Sanger, *An Autobiography,* New York: W. W. Norton and Company, 1938, pp. 254-255.

[3] Arnold W. Green, *Sociology,* New York: McGraw-Hill Book Company, 1952, p. 512.

[4] Max Weber, *The Theory of Social and Economic Organization* (translated by A. M. Henderson and Talcott Parsons), New York: Oxford University Press, 1947, p. 371. The characterization of legal leadership and its accompanying bureaucracy is also from Weber, Chapter III.

[5] H. G. Barnett, *Innovation: The Basis of Cultural Change,* New York: McGraw-Hill Book Company, 1953, p. 7.

[6] A. G. Keller, *Societal Evolution* (rev. ed.), New York: Macmillan Company, 1931, Chapter IV. The concept of

selection in the special and analytically valuable sense employed here is original with Keller.

[7] Ralph Linton, *The Study of Man,* New York: D. Appleton-Century, 1936, p. 272.

CHAPTER 4

[1] H. G. Barnett, *Innovation: The Basis of Cultural Change,* New York: McGraw-Hill Book Company, 1953, p. 379.

[2] *Ibid.,* pp. 381-404.

[3] William I. Thomas, ed., *Source Book for Social Origins,* Chicago: University of Chicago Press, 1909, pp. 16-18. See also Hadley Cantril, *The Psychology of Social Movements,* New York: John Wiley and Sons, 1941, p. 63. "Crisis" is here used in a somewhat narrower and more specific sense than that employed by Thomas or Cantril.

[4] H. van B. Cleveland *et al, The Theory of Social Tensions,* Washington, D. C.: Unpublished Manuscript, 1948, p. 5. These are the attributes of what is called in the manuscript social "cramp" rather than crisis.

[5] Barnett, *op. cit.,* p. 80.

[6] A. B. Wolfe, *Conservatism, Radicalism, and the Scientific Method,* New York: Macmillan Company, 1923, pp. 136-137.

[7] Arnold W. Green, *Sociology,* New York: McGraw-Hill Book Co., 1952, p. 489.

CHAPTER 5

[1] Ralph Linton, ed., *Acculturation in Seven American Indian Tribes,* New York: D. Appleton-Century Co., 1940, p. 474.

[2] Alvin W. Gouldner, ed., *Studies in Leadership,* New York: Harper and Brothers, 1950, pp. 57-64. The concepts of agitator and bureaucrat used in the present study are similar to Gouldner's, although they were formulated independently.

[3] Charles Hunt Page, "Bureaucracy's Other Face," *Social Forces,* Vol. 25 (1946), pp. 89-92. This article analyzes a similar development within the United States Navy.

[4] Philip Selznick, "An Approach to a Theory of Bureaucracy," *American Sociological Review,* Vol. 9 (1943), p. 51.

[5] Gouldner, *op. cit.,* p. 65.

[6] *Loc. cit.*

[7] Alfred McClung Lee, "Techniques of Social Reform: An Analysis of the New Prohibition Drive," *American Sociological Review,* Vol. 9 (1944), pp. 65-77. A rather extensive classification of functionaries is employed in this article.

[8] Linton, *op. cit.,* p. 473.

[9] Arnold W. Green, *Sociology,* New York; McGraw-Hill Book Company, 1952, p. 520.

[10] H. G. Barnett, *Innovation: The Basis of Cultural Change,* New York: McGraw-Hill Book Co., 1953, pp. 322-327.

[11] Rilma Buckman, "Social Engineering: A Study of the Birth Control Movement," *Social Forces,* Vol. 22 (1944), p. 424.

[12] Margaret Sanger, *An Autobiography,* New York: W. W. Norton and Co., 1938, pp. 393-395.

[13] Herbert Blumer, "Elementary Collective Behavior," *New Outline of the Principles of Sociology* (Alfred McClung Lee, ed.), New York: Barnes and Noble, 1951, pp. 206-207.

[14] Theodore Abel, "The Pattern of a Successful Political Movement," *American Sociological Review,* Vol. 2 (1937), p. 351.

[15] J. Stewart Burgess, "The Study of Modern Social Movements as a Means for Clarifying the Process of Social Action," *Social Forces,* Vol. 22 (1944), p. 274.

[16] Marcus Bach, *They Have Found a Faith,* Indianapolis: Bobbs-Merrill Co., 1946, p. 140.

CHAPTER 6

[1] Robin M. Williams, Jr., *American Society,* New York: Alfred A. Knopf, 1952, p. 388.

[2] Melville J. Herskovits, *Man and His Works,* New York: Alfred A. Knopf, 1949, p. 581. Though used increasingly by other writers, the concept of drift seems to have originated with Herskovits as an adaption from Sapir's work in linguistics.

[3] Joseph K. Johnson, *Christian Science: A Case Study of Religion As a Form of Adjustive Behavior,* St. Louis: Publications of Washington University, 1938, p. 6.

[4] Rudolf Heberle, *Social Movements,* New York: Appleton-Century-Crofts, 1951, p. 456.

[5] Herskovits, *op. cit.,* p. 553.

[6] H. G. Barnett, *Innovation: The Basis of Cultural Change,* New York: McGraw-Hill Book Co., 1953, p. 334.

[7] Marcus Bach, *They Have Found a Faith,* Indianapolis: Bobbs-Merrill, 1946, pp. 124-126.

[8] Theodore K. Noss, *Resistance to Social Innovation as Found in the Literature Regarding Innovations Which Have Proved Successful,* Chicago: University of Chicago Press, 1944, pp. 250-251.

[9] R. M. MacIver and Charles H. Page, *Society,* New York: Rinehart & Co., 1949, p. 223.

[10] Ralph Linton, ed., *Acculturation in Seven American Indian Tribes,* New York: D. Appleton-Century Co., 1940, p. 472.

[11] *Ibid.,* p. 473.

[12] Robert K. Merton, *Social Theory and Social Structure,* Glencoe, Ill.: Free Press, 1949, p. 51.

[13] David G. Mandelbaum, "Culture Change Among the Nilgiri Tribes," American Anthropologist, Vol. 43 (1941), p. 21.

[14] Ralph Linton, "Foreword" in Abram Kardiner, *The Individual and Society,* New York: Columbia University Press, 1939, p. xi.

[15] Wilson D. Wallis, *Culture and Progress,* New York: McGraw-Hill Book Co., 1930, pp. 114-115.

[16] MacIver and Page, *op. cit.,* p. 359.

[17] *Ibid.,* pp. 369-370.

[18] Barnett, *op. cit.,* pp. 314-317.

[19] MacIver and Page, *op. cit.,* p. 372. Reprinted with the publisher's permission.

[20] Williams, *op. cit.,* pp. 386-387.

[21] Theodore Abel, "The Patterns of a Successful Political Movement," *American Sociological Review,* Vol. 2 (1937), p. 349. Whereas Abel distinguishes between social and *personal* values, the comparison made here is between social, that is, society-wide, and *subgroup* values.

[22] Merton, *op. cit.,* p. 50.

[23] Noss, *op. cit.,* pp. 240-241.

[24] *Ibid.,* p. 250.

[25] Bernhard J. Stern, *Social Factors in Medical Progress,* New York: Columbia University Press, 1927, p. 11.

[20] Bernhard J. Stern, *Society and Medical Progress,* Princeton: Princeton University Press, 1941, Chapter IX.

CHAPTER 7

[1] William Graham Sumner, *Essays of William Graham Sumner* (A. G. Keller and Maurice R. Davie, *eds.*), New Haven: Yale University Press, 1934, pp. 11-19.

[2] David G. Mandelbaum, "Culture Change Among the Nilgiri Tribes," *American Anthropologist,* Vol. 43 (1941), p. 23.

[3] Melvile J. Herskovits, *Man and His Works,* New York: Alfred A. Knopf, 1949, p. 588.

[4] A. G. Keller, *Societal Evolution,* New York: Macmillan Co., 1931, p. 146.

[5] John M. Mecklin, *The Ku Klux Klan,* New York: Harcourt Brace and Co., 1924, p. 71.

[6] Sara Harris, *Father Divine: Holy Husband,* Garden City: Doubleday and Company, 1953, p. 45.

[7] Robert K. Merton, *Social Theory and Social Structure,* Glencoe, Ill.: Free Press, 1949, Chapter I.

[8] Philip Selznick, "An Approach to a Theory of Bureaucracy," *American Sociological Review,* Vol. 8 (1943), p. 49.

[9] Thomas H. Greer, *American Social Reform Movements,* New York: Prentice-Hall, 1949, p. 69.

[10] Solon Buck, *The Agrarian Crusade,* New Haven: Yale University Press, 1920, p. 71.

[11] Leonard W. Doob, *The Plans of Men,* New Haven: Yale University Press, 1940, p. 47.

[12] Arnold W. Green, *Sociology,* New York: McGraw-Hill Book Co., 1952, p. 506.

[13] H. G. Barnett, *Innovation: The Basis of Cultural Change,* New York: McGraw-Hill Book Co., 1953, p. 362.

SELECTED READINGS

General Sources

BARNETT, H. G., *Innovation: The Basis of Cultural Change,*
New York: McGraw-Hill Book Co., 1953.

Although peripheral to the subject at hand in some ways,
this study has a fundamental relevance for movements and
other related areas. Probably the most important work pub-
lished in the field of social change in over twenty years.

BLUMER, HERBERT, "Collective Behavior" in Lee, Alfred
McClung (*ed.*): *New Outline of the Principles of Sociology,*
Barnes and Noble, 1951.

This chapter is one of the most widely quoted sources on
social movements. Among its numerous useful insights those
on internal elements especially have been incorporated in
the present study, Chapter Two.

CANTRIL, HADLEY, *The Psychology of Social Movements,*
New York: John Wiley and Sons, 1941.

The first section of 75 pages is theoretical, stressing individual motivation and action; the second section contains good
descriptions and analyses of such movements as the Nazi
Party, the Oxford Group, Father Divine, and the Townsend
Plan.

GOULDNER, ALVIN W., ed., *Studies in Leadership,* New
York: Harper and Brothers, 1950.

Diverse in their points of view, here are some of the most
thoughtful essays available on leadership. Gouldner's intro-
ductions to the several sections are particularly cogent.

GREEN, ARNOLD W., *Sociology,* New York: McGraw-Hill
Book Co., 1952.

An interesting analysis of movements is contained in Chapter
24 along with an entertaining description of the Townsend
Plan and Moral Rearmament.

GREER, THOMAS H., *American Social Reform Movements,*
New York: Prentice-Hall, 1949.

A short and very competent history of major post-Civil War
reform efforts in the political and economic areas.

HEBERLE, RUDOLF, *Social Movements,* New York: Apple-ton-Century-Crofts, 1951.

A scholarly work containing an especially interesting section on the ecology of movements, which are viewed chiefly as an area of political sociology.

KELLER, A. G., *Societal Evolution,* New York: Macmillan Co., 1931.

Like Barnett's book, this one is tangential to the subject of movements but is recommended for its clear and incisive analysis of innovation and selection.

MERTON, ROBERT K., *Social Theory and Social Structure,* Glencoe, Ill.: Free Press, 1949.

The first essay is a lucid and essential statement on purposes and consequences in social action, distinguishing between kinds of consequences with the terms manifest function, latent function, and dysfunction.

WASHBURNE, NORMAN F., *Interpreting Social Change in America* (Short Studies in Sociology), New York, Random House, 1954.

A realistic treatment of social change with brief but illuminating references to social movements.

WILSON, LOGAN and KOLB, WILLIAM L., *Sociological Analysis,* New York: Harcourt, Brace and Co., 1949.

In Chapter 23 are three revealing articles on social change and movements by Theodore Abel, Alfred McClung Lee, and Rudolf Heberle.

Sources on specific movements frequently cited in this study

BACH, MARCUS, *They Have Found a Faith,* Indianapolis: Bobbs-Merrill Company, 1946.

Nine innovations in religion—including Father Divine's Kingdom and Moral Rearmament—are described with little bias and much interest, the latter stemming in part from the author's personal contacts with each faith.

BATES, ERNEST S., and DITTEMORE, JOHN V., *Mary Baker Eddy,* New York: Alfred A. Knopf, 1932.

Like all biographies of Mrs. Eddy, this one lacks objectivity but serves as a critical and detailed antidote for strongly partisan studies. It does not treat the movement's post-Eddy period.

BUCK, SOLON, *The Agrarian Crusade,* New Haven: Yale University Press, 1920.

Despite their vintage, the chapters on the Grange are as good as can be found anywhere on the movement and its social setting.

HARRIS, SARA, *Father Divine: Holy Husband,* Garden City, Doubleday and Company, 1953.

An ill-organized but instructive account of the Peace Mission Movement and its founder. Despite the lack of sociological orientation, descriptions seem accurate and appraisals unemotional.

HORN, S. F., *Invisible Empire,* New York: Harcourt, Brace and Co., 1939.

Devoted exclusively to the first Ku Klux Klan, this is a detailed yet readable narration of the movement's career during the years 1866-1871.

MECKLIN, JOHN M., *The Ku Klux Klan,* New York: Harcourt, Brace and Co., 1924.

Here are combined an objective, sober analysis of the second Klan and a realistic interpretation of its social context.

POWELL, LYMAN P., *Mary Baker Eddy,* New York: Macmillan Co., 1930.

The treatment of both Christian Science and its founder is distinctly sympathetic, almost fulsomely so. Yet this is probably the best of the works whose position is "pro" and is a good companion volume to critical books like Bates and Dittemore's.

SANGER, MARGARET, *An Autobiography,* New York: W. W. Norton and Co., 1938.

This remains the best single source on the otherwise poorly documented movement for birth control in the United States. Rich in social as well as personal detail.

TAYLOR, CARL C., *The Farmers' Movement: 1620-1920,* New York: American Book Co., 1953.

A respected rural sociologist turns in this volume to social history, and the result is a scholarly, sound picture of the Grange and many other farm movements.

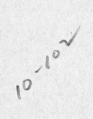

10-10